A CONCISE HISTORY OF

Spain

D1543224

A CONCISE HISTORY OF
Spain

HENRY KAMEN

*with 168 illustrations
and 4 maps*

CHARLES SCRIBNER'S SONS

NEW YORK

Frontispiece: detail of Goya's *The
Third of May 1808* (1814)

1 3 5 7 9 11 13 15 17 19 I/C 20 18 16 14 12 10 8 6 4 2

Printed in Great Britain
Library of Congress Catalog card Number 74-982

ISBN 0-684-13850-6

Contents

angelus sedet sup
nubem nubeum

ubi metitur   messem arere

ubi uindemiatur   bouos ur dicer carne

ubi calcatum est cor
cidur sanc   un calcate terra
sanguis usq ad frenof equo rum

ou auf

Foundations

For the ancients, Hispania was the edge of the world. The passage between the Pillars of Hercules (the modern Straits of Gibraltar) led out, poets explained, to an impassable sea of darkness. The Iberian peninsula therefore became the final destination of all the great expansionist civilizations.

The origins of the first settlers are obscure. Neanderthal man, as known in the peninsula, was rapidly displaced in the Palaeolithic period by immigrants from the north, from Africa and the eastern Mediterranean. These early arrivals left widely scattered traces of their work, showing them to be intelligent weapon-makers and active hunters. We can still see what their art was like in the many cave-paintings on the Levant coast and notably in the magnificent murals in the cave at Altamira (Santander). From about 3000 BC the primitive hunting habits of the inhabitants gave way, under the influence of new settlers, to a more domesticated culture. The use of copper and bronze, the domestication of animals, and reliance on agriculture, distinguished the transition from the Neolithic period to that of Bronze Age man. By the first millennium before Christ it is possible to locate definite races, mostly of African origin, in possession of specific areas of the peninsula. The Ligurians (north) and the Iberians (south and east) were the chief among these. Later, in about the seventh century BC, the Celts came from across the Pyrenees and dispersed over a large part of the peninsula. They tended to merge with the native peoples, and both are therefore commonly described as Celtiberians.

A new stage in the settlement of Iberia during the pre-Christian centuries was reached with the arrival of colonists from the trans-Mediterranean civilizations. First came the Phoenicians in about the eighth century BC. They came mainly to trade, but ended by settling in what is modern Andalucia, where they founded Gadir (modern Cadiz) and other colonies and built up a highly civilized and peaceful culture in Tartessos, the Tarshish of the Bible. They were followed about a century later by the Greeks, who implanted themselves in the south and along the Mediterranean coast. The principal Greek settlement was in Emporion, on the Catalan seaboard, but Greek culture and trading interests extended more widely. The first coins in the peninsula were minted by the Greeks, and they also introduced two

The Lord's Harvest, a leaf from an eleventh-century copy of the commentary on the Apocalypse of St John. The commentary, written by Beatus of Liebana only a few decades after the Muslim conquest of Spain, is a profound and enduring work of Christian scholarship; the illuminated versions made three centuries later are some of the most brilliant examples of Mozarabic art, and form a valuable record of contemporary life.

plants that were to be of fundamental importance in Spanish history, the olive and the vine. A few remnants of Greek culture, mainly statues, have been found. Merging with native influences, the style produced outstanding Graeco-Iberian sculpture, of which one example, the haunting figure of the Lady of Elche, is the most distinguished piece of work to survive from Levantine art of the fifth century BC.

In this century the Phoenician colony at Carthage in North Africa began to expand into Iberian territory. Tradition says that the Phoenicians of Cadiz called Carthage in to help them against Tartessos. This was not the last time that the destinies of the peninsula were to be changed by calling in outsiders. The Carthaginians quickly took over and exploited the areas colonized by their predecessors. Their hold on Iberian territory was to be indispensable, for the rising tide of rivalry between Rome and Carthage soon drove them to rely heavily on the resources of the peninsula. The main achievement of Carthage seems then to have been to induce the conquering Romans to come in as well.

What brought so many waves of settlers to Iberia? Much of the land is by nature harsh and uninviting. Immigrants coming through the Pyrenees encountered, if they struck westward, an occasionally rugged but well-watered area suitable for crops and grazing. Striking eastward, they came out into hospitable land with good harbours for trade. But farther inland there were arid expanses unsuited to comfortable settlement, and beyond that the land rose steeply into the dry wastes of the central *meseta*, inhabited exclusively by the primitive tribes of the peninsula. The newcomers therefore tended to remain on

Above, limestone figure of the Dame de El Cerro de los Santos, fifth or fourth century BC, found in 1897 near Albacete.

Right, sixth- or fifth-century BC gold ear-ring from Caceres in western Spain. The goldsmith's intricate technique owes much to Etruscan and Phoenician craftsmanship.

Opposite, the Lady of Elche, one of the best-known and most controversial examples of Iberian art of the fifth and fourth centuries BC. Her serenity recalls classical models, her elaborate attire, the native tradition.

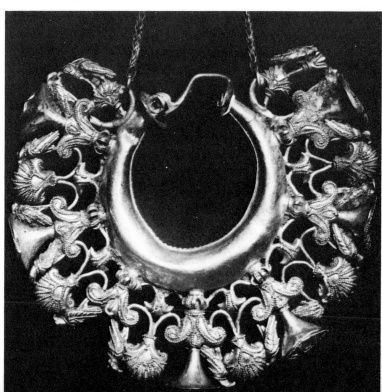

the periphery, where both agriculture and mining were possible. Settlers from Africa and the eastern Mediterranean likewise restricted themselves to the southern littoral and the rich river valleys. They were particularly attracted by the low-lying coastlands along the Mediterranean.

Most of the significant cultural remains of ancient Iberia are located in these peripheral areas. Strabo, who complained of the inhospitable central *meseta*, could speak in contrast of the 'gentility and culture' of Tartessos, of its art and poetry. The Greeks of Emporion were likewise diligent guardians of the artistic heritage of their race, as we can see from the striking classical statues discovered in their area. Later colonizers remained in these outer territories and refused to be drawn inland. The Carthaginians, who were the first to attempt any serious conquest of the peninsula, were no exception. They occupied the southern and eastern coastlands, basing themselves on cities such as Cadiz and New Carthage (modern Cartagena). Despite a carefully organized policy of settlement, the Carthaginians continued to suffer the hostility both of the natives of the interior and of the Romans who were extending their influence southwards.

The Second Punic War (third century BC) between Carthage and Rome destroyed the power of the former in Iberia. The Carthaginian leader Hamilcar Barca began the systematic use of the peninsula as a military base. His son Hannibal successfully conquered the Mediterranean coastal lands, crossed the Ebro (the dividing line between Roman and Carthaginian spheres of control, agreed in 226 BC) and marched into Gaul, towards Italy. His brilliant campaigns in Italy after a magnificent crossing of the Alps forced the Romans to open a second front in Hispania. Roman forces there were put under the command of the Scipio family. It was P. Cornelius Scipio who finally carried out the destruction of Carthaginian power. Cartagena fell to him in 209 B C; Cadiz was handed over three years later.

The failure of the Carthaginians to dominate Iberia was caused in part by geographical hindrances to unity in the peninsula. The Cantabrian Mountains in the north, the high plateau of the Castilian *meseta* in the centre, the Sierra Morena in the south, served to divide rather than unite, to hinder conquest and integration rather than facilitate it. The sharp contrast between rich agricultural land on the northern and north-eastern littoral and dry grazing-land in the south and interior emphasized the economic divisions in the peninsula. The Carthaginians were unable to overcome these factors, and remained essentially a coastal power. Hannibal's only important expedition inland, to Salamanca, was abortive.

The absorption of Iberia into the Roman Empire ushered it into one of its greatest cultural periods. Roman domination lasted from

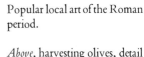

Popular local art of the Roman period.

Above, harvesting olives, detail of a relief from a Roman sarcophagus from Córdoba (*c.* 200 BC), and a relief symbolizing summer (*aestas*) (sixth – seventh century AD).

Left, tombstone commemorating the death of Amaransis, wife of Victor, an innkeeper, at the age of forty-five; the relief shows her drawing a flagon of wine (third or fourth century AD).

roughly the second century BC to the early fifth century AD. In these seven centuries of fairly regular peace and order the peninsula – Hispania, the Romans called it – underwent a fundamental transformation. The conquest was not easy, and never total. Resistance by the Lusitanians (Portugal) and by the Celtiberians (Castile) preoccupied Roman forces in the second century BC. The peoples of Catalonia were so stubborn in revolt that Livy described them as *ferox genus*, a fierce people. The fall of the Celtiberian city of Numantia to Scipio Aemilianus in 133 BC marks the end of any serious opposition to Rome. In the north, the Asturians and Cantabrians were not subdued till the personal intervention of Augustus Caesar himself (29–19 BC).

The Romans divided the subdued territory into two separate provinces, Farther Hispania and Hither Hispania, roughly west and east respectively of the River Ebro. Later these divisions were amplified. The beginning of the civil wars in Rome made several generals realize how important a bastion of power Hispania could be. The first century BC thus saw the entry into the peninsula of the forces of both Pompey and Julius Caesar. On the creation of the Empire under Augustus, Hispania was recognized as a vital province. An intensive period of pacification and Romanization now began.

For the first, and arguably the last, time some sort of political and moral unity was imposed on Hispania. The inhabitants of the peninsula were referred to collectively as Hispani. It is possible to consider the Roman achievement as no more than the imposition of external force upon the customs and culture of the natives. But these were soon encouraged to identify themselves with the habits of their conquerors. The fruits of the soil and the mines made Hispania into an important trading nation, roads were constructed (to a total of some thirteen thousand miles), a common coinage was introduced. The great aqueducts at Segovia, Tarragona and Mérida – three widely separated cities – still bear witness today to the practical work of the conquerors in building cities and supplying them with essential services. Tarragona in particular was an outstanding provincial capital, described by Strabo as 'supplied with all necessities, no less frequented than Carthage, metropolis of the greater part of Hispania'. Roman economic interests exploited the rich natural resources of the mines in gold, silver, iron and lead; olive oil and Hispanic wine entered the Mediterranean market. Thanks to the co-operation of the landed and urban upper classes, Roman habits and culture became widely accepted. Privileges, notably that of becoming a citizen of Rome, were extended to the Hispano-Roman patriciate. Roman social divisions, into freemen and slaves, were adopted. A highly privileged class of estate-owners, some from the native aristocracy and others from the Roman élite, was

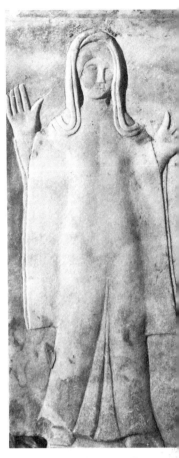

Praying figure from a fifth-century Christian sarcophagus at Tarragona.

The Roman aqueduct at Segovia, built by the Emperor Trajan (AD 98–117) of granite blocks fitted together without cement.

13

confirmed in possession of large tracts of arable land. These big estates (*latifundia*), sometimes worked by slave labour, marked the beginning of the system of feudal landholding. The Latin language became the official tongue of the Hispanic population. Most significantly of all in the long term, Christianity filtered through under the Empire.

The socio-political impact of Rome was perhaps the most profound. The impressive ruins at Italica (Seville) and Mérida represent the triumph of urban civilization in a semi-barbaric environment. Whatever Rome had to offer came principally from the cities, few and scattered as they were, though none the less permanent guarantors of Hispanic culture. The country estates, so beloved of retired poets and statesmen, were likewise fated to be an element of continuity, for they initiated the pattern, continued down to today, of extensive rural areas and industries, exploited by a narrow élite and worked by depressed labourers. The significance of the cultural impact, though important, is far more doubtful. Hispania was the cradle of some of the greatest names in later Latin literature, of Seneca and Lucan, of Quintilian and Martial, of Pomponius Mela the geographer and Marcus Portius Cato the tutor of Ovid. It also produced four emperors, among them Trajan and Hadrian. But few of the writers, even those with Iberian blood such as Martial, could be said to reflect an unmistakably Hispanic outlook: all were Romans. It was not yet time for the peninsula to make a distinctive contribution; it remained still a recipient of alien cultures. Surviving Roman sculpture of up to the fourth century AD shows (unlike Greek remains) almost no trace of a dilution with native influences. The Hispania that the Romans celebrated was merely a colony, an elegant retreat, a supplier of wines and precious metals. For Pliny the Levant coast was, after Italy and the fabled Indies, the most excellent place in the world for 'its ardour in work, the energy of its slaves, the bodily endurance of its people, and their vehement spirit'.

The continuity of Roman culture in its epoch of decadence was assured by the rise of Christianity. St Paul brought the seeds to the peninsula and they struck root readily in the thirsty soil of a culture lacking in mystical ideals. As a dissident minority religion, Christianity was persecuted sporadically, and numerous Hispanic martyrs soon joined the calendar of saints. By its acceptance among the non-official sectors of society, the new religion assured itself a continued existence even when the framework of imperial authority was being rejected. At the same time the Church adopted a diocesan organization which paralleled the official structure and so by association became part of the temporal order. By the fourth century, Hispanic and Roman Christianity were intimately intertwined. The peninsula which had given emperors to Rome now gave popes: St Damasus,

Pope from AD 366 to 384, was a Catalan. Many other Christians distinguished themselves in the universal Church: Hosius, Bishop of Cordoba, acted as president of the Council of Nicaea; Priscillian, Bishop of Avila, had the misfortune to be burnt for heresy. Among the most memorable believers of the fourth century was the great Christian poet Prudentius, a Hispanic gentleman who at the age of fifty-seven renounced the world and entered the cloister. There he composed some of the most intense religious lyrics of early Latin Christianity.

In the late third century AD the peninsula became the object of raiding expeditions, in the north by the Franks who penetrated into the Catalan provinces and in the south by the Moors who made incursions into Andalucia. Then in AD 409, a year before the Visigothic leader Alaric sacked Rome, several Germanic tribes swept through Gaul and poured over the Pyrenees into Hispania. The tall, blond 'barbarian' nomads, contemptuous of the urbanized civilization of the Romans, were composed principally of the Suevi, Vandals and Alans. From 415 onwards the Visigoths also extended their operations to the peninsula. Under the Visigothic ruler Theodoric II (453–66) the opposition of the barbarians within Hispania was largely obliterated and the Visigoths began to control the peninsula independently of Roman authority.

Visigothic rule continued until the Muslim invasions in the early eighth century. In these three centuries Hispanic society underwent important changes. The Hispano-Roman population, though still the majority group, was scattered and fragmented. One consequence was that the major cities, which had been the nucleus of its culture, began to decline. The Germanic population remained an unabsorbed minority living in rural settlements rather than in cities. Divisions between Hispano-Romans and Visigoths went deep. The former were a cultured patriciate, living in cities, well endowed with land, Catholic in religion. The latter were a warlike nomadic race based on a tribal structure, largely unlettered, eschewing urban life, and Arian Christian in religion. These important differences were aggravated by the presence of yet another religious division: a large and growing colony of Jews, who were severely persecuted throughout the Visigothic period. Religious disunity among Christians was officially eliminated by the conversion of King Recared from Arianism to Catholicism at a public ceremony during the Third Council of Toledo (589). But racial and social disunity could not be so easily cured, and the political disputes provoked by the Visigothic principle of elective kingship led eventually to a major quarrel that brought the Muslims into Hispania.

The Visigothic achievement was tenuous. Because of their relatively primitive cultural level the Visigoths left little by way of art or

Opposite, leaf from the tenth-century *Codex Vigilanus* depicting the later Visigothic monarchs and, beneath them, the first rulers of the northern Christian kingdom of León. On the bottom row are portraits of other court officials.

Above, late seventh-century Visigothic relief from Burgos showing Christ between two angels.

Left, interior of the ninth-century church of Santa Cristina de Lena in Asturias, the tiny Visigothic stronghold in the north of Spain.

17

buildings. Intellectual leadership was supplied by the Hispanic élite and by the Catholic clergy. 'They were the ones', we are told, 'who shaped the legislation, the spiritual life, and the relative economic splendour of the Visigothic monarchy during the seventh century.' St Isidore of Seville (560–636) was the spiritual giant of this era. The Visigoths did not create a strong political structure, but they bequeathed a valuable code of their laws, the *Liber Judiciorum* (654), which served as a guide to subsequent legislators of Christian Hispania. Already in these laws we see the beginnings of the system of social relationships that developed into feudalism.

In 711 an Arab-Berber army entered the peninsula as an ally of the pretender to the Visigothic throne. There are various accounts of how this event came about, all reflecting bitter rivalry among the Christians. The invading troops disembarked at a point which came to be called, after one of their generals, Jabal-Tariq (Gibraltar) or the Mountain of Tariq. The troops of the last Visigothic King, Rodrigo, were defeated at the Battle of Guadalete and the King killed. In the course of the next seven years most of the peninsula fell under Moorish control, as the foreign allies slowly transformed themselves into conquerors. Their rapid success may be explained partly by the welcome given to them by opponents of the Visigothic monarchy, but also by the structural weaknesses of the Visigothic state. Islamic domination of Hispania, which reached its zenith at the end of the tenth century, had begun.

Resistance continued in the hardy north-west, principally in the region of Asturias. The nucleus of opposition can be traced to a Christian chieftain called Pelayo, whose first stronghold was the cave of Covadonga in the Asturian mountains and who claimed to be a descendant of the Visigothic kings. Muslim failure to subdue the resisters was in the long run to prove fatal. The Christian kingdom of Asturias, which extended along the Galician and Cantabrian coasts (a region that had always been the most difficult for invaders to conquer), maintained an independent existence, welcomed refugees from the Muslim-dominated lands, and assumed the role of defender of Christian civilization in the peninsula. Some support to its claims to leadership of the Christians was supplied by the legend of St James (Santiago). In the ninth century the Christians of Galicia were convinced that they had discovered the body of St James the Apostle. A shrine was erected, and the Saint soon came to be regarded as the patron of the struggle against the Moors. As his fame spread, the shrine at Compostela became the greatest centre of pilgrimage in western Europe. Soldiers engaged in battle with the Muslims swore time and again that they had seen the Saint riding before them to victory on a white horse.

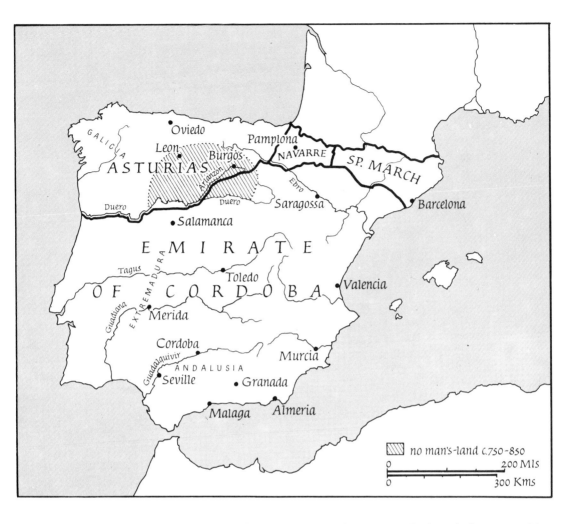

Under the sway of Visigothic rulers, the Asturians established a powerful little enclave that gradually tried to extend itself, encroaching on the no-man's-land separating it from the Moorish territories. In addition to Asturias, the Pyrenees were the home of several principalities which in the eighth century recognized the suzerainty of the Frankish rulers. Ever since the Franks had blocked the northward expansion of the Moors by defeating them at Poitiers in 732, they had taken over the defence of the Pyrenees. Attempts by the Frankish ruler Charlemagne to press the struggle into the peninsula were checked by a defeat of some of his forces at Saragossa. When retreating through the Pyrenees after this reversal, their rearguard was attacked in the pass of Roncesvalles, an episode immortalized and elaborated upon in the legendary *Song of Roland*. Despite the incident, Charlemagne managed to consolidate Frankish control over the northern counties, known collectively as the Hispanic March.

Spain at the beginning of the ninth century.

The Arab invasion brought new aesthetic ideas and sophisticated techniques. The most important surviving architectural example is the Grand Mosque at Córdoba (begun in 785, extended in the tenth century and converted after the Reconquest into a cathedral). The double horseshoe arches of the sanctuary (*opposite*) are a typical element of the Hispano-Arab style.

Left, twelfth-century textile fragment from Andalucia. The Arabic inscription reads 'perfect blessings'.

Below, tenth-century ivory casket with silver-gilt mounts from Córdoba. The inscription is to one of the daughters of Caliph Abd-ar-Rahman III.

Hispano-Mauresque tile, its intricate design evidence of the skill of Arab ceramists in the ninth and tenth centuries.

The first three hundred years of the Muslim conquest gave Hispania a unique character among west European countries. Save for the Pyrenean regions and the territory to the north of the River Duero (which in effect was the kingdom of Asturias), the entire land mass was subjected by and received the imprint of Islamic civilization. Three centuries of virtually undisputed Muslim rule gave Hispania its indelibly Moorish characteristics.

Spain's Moorish past is so readily accepted by the modern traveller that it requires some effort to grasp the scale of the revolution that over-took the peninsula. A wholly foreign race professing a strongly hostile religion took over the country, a totally alien language became the official tongue, a completely novel culture was imposed on the population. Entire sections of the peasantry and the urban élite deserted their Catholic faith and embraced Islam. By the tenth century the territory called Al-Andalus was a country with a solid Muslim majority, and had become the single most powerful and civilized state in western Europe. The Moorish state was never so integrated or unified that it crushed out the cultures that had preceded it. None the less, Islamic culture itself became so imbedded in the Hispanic mentality that it ceased to be alien and became an ineffaceable and authentic part of peninsular history.

The subjected Christian population was usually treated with the limited religious tolerance customary to Islam. Occasional persecution was matched by outbreaks of religious zeal on the part of the conquered. Those who held fast to their faith were called Mozarabs, Christian in belief but Arabized in culture and language. Their numbers, however, shrank, and their faith itself became diluted with novel beliefs and heresies. Many were attracted by the higher quality of Islamic culture. 'Alas,' lamented a ninth-century Córdoban, 'all the young Christians who become notable for their talents know only the language and literature of the Arabs, read and study Arabic books with zeal, and everywhere proclaim aloud that their literature is worthy of admiration.' The principal episcopal see, Toledo, once the Visigothic capital, found itself isolated as the sees of the Christian north freed themselves from its jurisdiction. Despite these drawbacks, Mozarabism remained a vitally important phenomenon. It represented a profound dialogue between Muslim and Christian civilization, and retained enough of an identity to prepare the way for an eventual re-conversion of the lands which the Muslims had made their own.

For the Arabs, Al-Andalus was only a province of the great empire of the Umayyad caliphs of Damascus. Abd-ar-Rahman (756–88), also a member of the Umayyad family, fled from the Abbasid caliphs when they overthrew the Umayyads in 750, and emerged finally in Al-Andalus as the new leader. It was he who established the emirate

The art of the Christian north. *Left*, ivory cross made for King Ferdinand of Castile in 1063; its animal design follows that of the Mozarabic south. *Below*, leaves from Beatus' commentary on the Apocalypse; such was the stylistic influence of Arab manuscripts that Jerusalem, the Heavenly City, is portrayed as a Moorish town.

of Córdoba and made it independent of the Abbasids in Damascus. Abd-ar-Rahman's successors in the emirate were largely concerned with stabilizing their power. This could be done ruthlessly, as in 818 when an uprising in Córdoba was followed by the execution of several hundreds of the surviving rebels. Not until the reign of Abd-ar-Rahman III (912–61) did the emirate reach what is commonly regarded as the peak of its splendour. After dealing with various dissident movements this ruler felt strong enough in 929 to proclaim himself Caliph and Commander of the Faithful, thereby asserting his equality with and independence of all other Islamic rulers.

The Umayyad caliphate in Spain was indubitably the greatest period of Al-Andalus. It was a civilization based principally on the towns, for the Muslims were primarily townspeople, as the Hispano-Romans had been. The high achievement of Al-Andalus in political administration and in civic culture, both based on the growth of large cities such as Córdoba and Granada, stands in clear contrast to the modest cultural level of the largely pastoral and rural northern Christian kingdoms. The towns also acted as thriving centres for the very active commerce the Moors developed: in oranges, figs, rice, sugar-cane, cotton and many other items, all of which they introduced into the peninsula for the first time. They exploited the rich mineral deposits of the south and built up flourishing industries in wool, silk, glass, paper, weapons, leather and so on. Fleets trading in these goods sold their merchandise as far afield as western Asia. Agricultural progress was furthered by extension of the very efficient irrigation works. The Muslim way of life made a profound impression on the Castilian and European vocabulary, as words denoting items and professions closely identified with the Arabs passed into common usage. Castilian words such as *alcázar* (castle), *aduana* (customs-house), *alcalde* (mayor), *arroz* (rice), *sandía* (water-melon) are typical of the thousands derived from the Arabic past. Words such as algebra, alcohol, orange, alchemy, sugar, lemon and aubergine passed into English use.

The last of the great masters of the Córdoban empire was Al-Mansur, chief minister and virtual ruler of the realm from 981 to 1002. Al-Mansur undertook the last great aggressive campaigns against the Christian princes of the north, with unequalled ferocity. He sacked Barcelona, attacked León and Coimbra, destroyed numerous monasteries, among them the church of St James at Compostela, and made a total of fifty-seven victorious expeditions against the powerless Christians. 'To Cordoba', writes a modern historian, 'came as trophy from the northern campaigns, crowds of prisoners and trains of carts loaded with the heads of the defeated or with crosses, sacred vessels and other precious booty. Christian captives laboured on the extension to the Great Mosque.' Christian kings sent him their daughters as wives or even as slaves. But the triumphs, although they established the supremacy of the caliphate virtually up to the Pyrenees, did not significantly alter the Christian-Muslim frontier, and indeed helped to weaken the financial stability of Córdoba. After Al-Mansur's death the caliphate fell into decay and confusion, in which discordant rivalries broke up the unity of the realm. In 1031 the caliphate formally ceased to exist. A régime of local rulers, the *reyes de taifas* or 'party kings', came into existence.

By the early eleventh century Al-Andalus had broken down into twenty-three independent political units, some regionally based, others the result of racial rivalry between Hispanic Muslims and immigrant Berbers. Some of these kingdoms were so weak that they inevitably became involuntary protectorates of their stronger Christian neighbours. One of the ablest Christian rulers, Alfonso VI of León and Castile (1065–1109), actually drew tribute from the *taifa* of Seville, and conquered Toledo permanently for the Christians in 1085. In the process, political links between Christians and Muslims became closer, and rivalries crossed the confessional barrier. The most celebrated military hero of this epoch, the Cid (from the Arabic *sayyid*, or lord), served both Christian and Muslim rulers. Celebrated in one of the most famous medieval romances, the *Poem of the Cid* (1140), his real name was Rodrigo Díaz de Vivar, a Castilian noble who in about 1081 transferred his services from Alfonso VI to the Muslim King of Saragossa. After several campaigns the Cid ended his career as independent ruler of the Muslim city of Valencia, which he captured in 1094. Despite his identification with the Muslims, he came to be looked upon by Christians as their ideal of a crusading warrior. No clearer example exists of the intertwining of the two civilizations, and their mutual understanding even in the face of war.

The Christian rulers in the north had by now resumed an aggressive role in the peninsula. For long overshadowed by Al-Andalus, only gradually did they emerge from its shadow. The realm of Asturias-León had been the earliest Christian nucleus. As it declined in vigour, leadership was taken over by Navarre, ruled at its zenith by Sancho III the Great (1000–35). Sancho eventually extended his dominions to include the whole of Castile and took in lands to the west as far as Barcelona. He defeated and subdued Leon, and enjoyed links with the rest of Christian Europe, largely thanks to the key position of Navarre athwart the great international pilgrims' road to the tomb of St James of Compostela. It is indicative of their relative weakness that the Christian princes of this period were more concerned with fighting each other than with combating the Muslims. But the Christian frontier took on new importance when Sancho III's son Ferdinand (1035–65) succeeded to the throne of Castile. A highly successful

King Ferdinand I of Castile: detail of a relief on the gilded silver shrine of St Isidore. Under Ferdinand's rule the first major successes in the Christian Reconquest of Spain were achieved.

soldier, Ferdinand I's campaigns involved the absorption and subordination of León and Navarre respectively, so that it was Castile which came to the forefront among the Christian powers in Hispania. His military expeditions went as far as Coimbra and Valencia at each extreme of the peninsula. Under his son, Alfonso VI, Castile established beyond question its leadership of the Christian cause.

Alfonso reunited the realms of Castile and León, received the homage of Aragon and Navarre, and crowned his achievements with the recovery of Toledo, the old Visigothic capital, from the Moors. The Castile that now emerged was made up of resolute frontiersmen who lived off the land which they had won for themselves or which the King had granted them. Ruler (after the capture of Toledo) of a Muslim minority and recipient of tribute from Arab kings in Al-Andalus, Alfonso now styled himself 'Emperor of the two religions' and even 'Emperor of all Spain'. At the same time, he brought his realms into line with the rest of Christian Europe. He made safe the famous pilgrims' way to the shrine of St James; thanks to him the monastic system of Cluny was introduced from France into the peninsula. Papal influence, now of increasing importance, led to a momentous change comparable to that which had occurred in England at the

Court life of the north. A musician and a warrior as they appear in a Beátus manuscript.

Synod of Whitby in 663. The Mozarabic rite, used by the Hispanic Church since the post-Roman era, was abandoned in favour of the Latin rite of the Roman Church. The change did not occur without considerable opposition, and we are told that only a miracle persuaded the court to accept the new rite. Missals of the two liturgies were subjected to an ordeal by fire. The Roman missal remained unconsumed in the flames. The Mozarabic missal leapt beyond the range of the fire, but the King thrust it back and declared for the Roman rite.

The triumphs of the Christians threw the southern rulers into despair. They appealed repeatedly for help from Africa. In response the fanatical Almoravids of the Sahara, fresh from the conquest of Morocco, crossed the Straits, entered the peninsula and inflicted a crushing defeat on Alfonso at Sagrajas, near Badajoz (1086). They returned to Africa after the expedition, but returned in 1090, and this time they stayed. By the end of the century they had subdued and united most of the *taifa* kingdoms, which were ushered into a period of religious intolerance. Life for the Jewish and Christian minority was made distinctly unpleasant by the intense religious strictness of the Almoravids. Their rule in Al-Andalus lasted till about 1145. They were then superseded by the invasion of another fanatical Berber tribe from

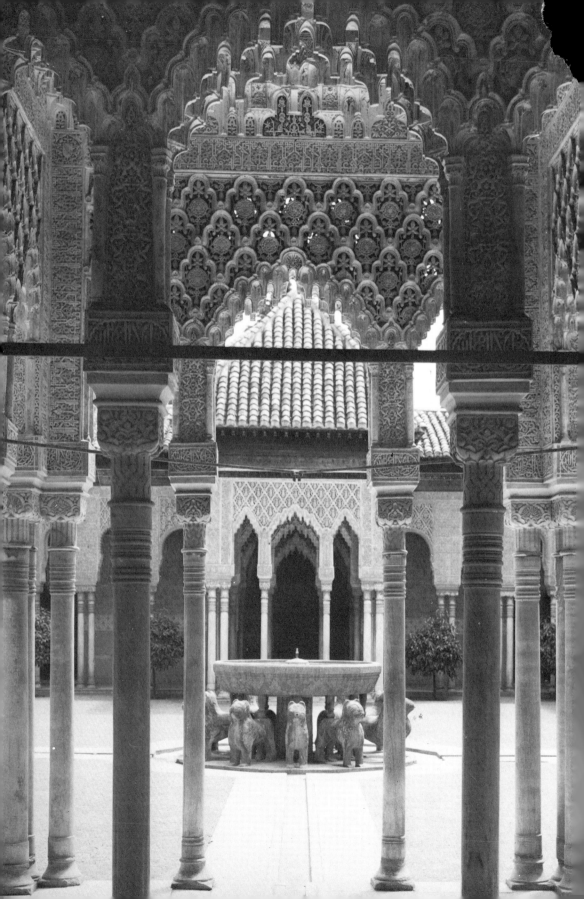

Morocco, the Almohads. From about 1170 onwards these even more intolerant Muslims assumed a leading role in Al-Andalus and added greater vigour to the struggle against the Christians. But the tide was turning against the decaying Arab principalities. In July 1212 a combined Christian force met the Almohads at Las Navas de Tolosa and shattered their power in the peninsula.

Most prominent among the memorials of the Moorish past are the great public monuments, of which the mosque at Córdoba is one of the earliest and most striking. Most surviving masterpieces date from the last period of Arab rule. The beautiful Giralda at Seville, originally the minaret of a mosque and subsequently the cathedral tower, dates from the time of the Almohads, as does the Torre del Oro on the river-banks of the same city. The master-work of Moorish artists, the Alhambra of Granada, acquired its most beautiful sections under the Nasrids in the late fourteenth century. Muslim culture thus reached its zenith only in the years of decline. What was true of public architecture was equally so of writing and thought, partly perhaps because the multiplicity of 'party kings' offered greater opportunities of patronage and more scope for expression. The language of Al-Andalus was Arabic, so understandably its written culture remains little known outside the Islamic world. This is a pity, since the Andalucian poets, for all their attention to the East, wrote and thought within an environment that was quite distinct. The eleventh century was the principal age of literary production, with scholar-poets like Ibn-Hazm. The twelfth century was distinguished by the writings of Averroes (Ibn-Rushd, d. 1198). Through Averroes and other Muslim philosophers and scientists the learning of the Greeks was transmitted, sometimes in a slightly distorted form, to western Europe. It was in the twelfth century too that Jewish savants were most active. Rabbi Ben Ezra (d. 1139) travelled abroad to the Christian countries. The greatest Jewish philosopher of the time, Maimonides (d. 1204), wrote his treatises in these years – in Arabic. In so far as the culture of Al-Andalus extended to North Africa, we may include as part of the Hispanic tradition the work of the distinguished historian Ibn-Khaldun (1332–1406), who spent a few years at Granada.

The material culture of Al-Andalus survived: the cities, the irrigation systems, the administrative machinery, the language, the folk-songs; but they were absorbed by and adapted to Christian usages. Later Islamic culture in its turn took on much that was Christian, and, being substantially more hybrid, must be looked at in a different context.

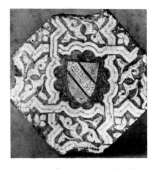

Opposite, the Courtyard of the Lions in the Alhambra of Granada, triumph of the final flowering of Muslim art in the late fourteenth century. *Above,* a wall-tile from the palace decorated with the shield of the Nasrid kings.

2

The Rise of Castile and Aragon

The outstanding feature of the thirteenth century in the peninsula was the progress of the *Reconquista*, or Reconquest. Co-operation between the major Christian powers was primarily responsible for the decisive victory over the Almohads at Las Navas de Tolosa in 1212. The century was to see the irresistible advance of Christian forces. In 1236 Córdoba fell, in 1246 Jaén, in 1248 Seville. In the eastern territories the island of Mallorca was taken in 1229, Valencia in 1238. Murcia was taken by Castilian forces in 1244. By the mid-thirteenth century Muslim power had been restricted exclusively to the southernmost part of Al-Andalus, the kingdom of Granada.

The Reconquest occupied several centuries and clearly plays a fundamental role in Hispanic history. It is not easy to define its nature. Christians appear to have considered it a just struggle to recover land that was rightfully theirs. This seems a curious view, since the Arabs had been in the peninsula for nearly seven centuries. But the religious motive was also important: Christian princes undoubtedly wished to defend their faith against the aggressive Almoravids and Almohads. At the same time military activity became one of the most important driving forces in society. The common herdsmen and shepherds of the Castilian frontier were as much the vanguard of the northern advance as the cowboys were in the American West. Distinction in warfare brought rewards and sometimes noble rank: it was to this militant nobility that the fruits of conquest fell. They obtained grants of land as well as the right to draw tribute and exact labour services from the subjected Muslim population. The military ethic and the struggle to extend the frontiers were given a higher sanction by the Christian religion. The notion of a crusade against the infidel, though not always predominant, was seldom absent from the enterprise, and endured for centuries in the Spanish mentality. The fusion of religious and military functions is best illustrated by the creation in the late twelfth century of three monastic orders of knights – the famous orders of Calatrava, Alcántara and Santiago – whose task was to defend the outposts bordering Muslim territory.

In the course of the gradual expansion of the frontier against Islam the Christian kingdoms acquired the form they were to take in the

St James of Compostela, patron of the long struggle to regain Spain for Christianity, depicted as the Moor-killer on a fifteenth-century marble statue from Compostela.

31

Opposite, James I of Aragon in battle against the Moors at Puig de Cebolla, 1235: detail from a late fourteenth-century Valencian altarpiece. St George, the soldier-saint, appears in the midst of the battle.

Left, troops from a Catalan naval expedition attacking the Palacio de Almudaina in Palma de Mallorca, 1229: detail of a contemporary wall-painting.

Catalan knights: detail of a wall-painting dating from about 1400.

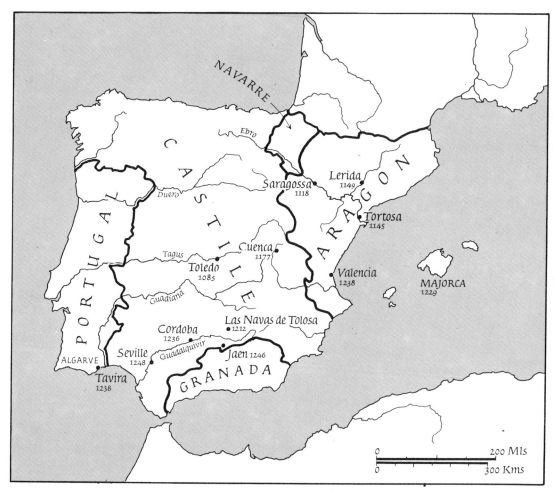

NAVARRE

CASTILE

ARAGON

PORTUGAL

GRANADA

Ebro

Saragossa
1118

Lerida
1149

Tortosa
1145

Duero

Tagus

Cuenca
1177

Toledo
1085

Valencia
1238

MAJORCA
1229

Guadiana

Las Navas de Tolosa
● 1212

Cordoba
1236

Guadalquivir

Jaen 1246

Seville
1248

ALGARVE

Tavira
1238

0   200 Mls

0   300 Kms

Map showing the kingdoms of Castile and Aragon and the gradual advance of Christianity in Spain. By the mid-thirteenth century only Granada remained under Muslim control, though the Reconquest was not completed until 1492, under Ferdinand and Isabella.

early modern period. By the middle of the twelfth century three main states were coming into being: Portugal, Castile and Aragon. Portugal reached its modern frontiers in 1238, when it completed the conquest of the Algarve, its southernmost territory. From this point it ceases to form part of our story, though inevitably it continued to influence the destinies of the peninsula.

The unity imposed on Castile by Alfonso VI did not last long. His defeat at the hands of the Almoravids began the break-up of the kingdom. One separatist movement in Galicia even tried to transfer that region to the sovereignty of William the Conqueror in England. Under Alfonso's successors all semblance of unity was lost. Alfonso VII, at his death in 1157, divided the realm by leaving Castile to his elder son Sancho and León to his younger son Ferdinand. The division was followed by internal conflicts and civil wars. In spite of this, Castile was moving towards external co-operation, the first real evidence being the agreements with the rulers of Barcelona, by which they joined forces for battle against the Moors and defined their respective spheres of expansion. Thanks to these agreements, Aragon helped in the campaigns to recover Cuenca (1177) and Murcia, but both these cities were incorporated into Castile. In return, Valencia was assured to the Aragonese and Catalans. Though internecine struggles continued in Christian territories, there was seldom any hesitation in co-operating for the struggle against Islam. The decisive period for Castile came with the reign of Ferdinand III (1217–52), later canonized as St Ferdinand. He initiated the most successful stage of the Castilian conquest of Andalucia, and under him the kingdom was extended to include Murcia in the east and Seville and Cadiz in the south. Castile had thus reached the Mediterranean and the Atlantic, and with the exception of the kingdom of Granada the Reconquest was complete. In 1230 Ferdinand also became ruler of León, when the two kingdoms were finally united under one crown. In possession now of a small navy, Castile prepared to push onwards into Africa, but the death of Ferdinand stopped this enterprise.

Just as the principality of Asturias-León had evolved into the unit that came to be called 'Castile', so the Pyrenean counties evolved towards the growth of 'Aragon'. Aragonese advance into the Muslim lands scored its most important gains in the twelfth century under Alfonso I the Warrior (1104–34). The capture of Saragossa (1118) gave the emergent Christian kingdom its historic capital. Both Castile from the west and the Catalans from the east sought closer links with the Aragonese. In 1135 Alfonso VII of Castile entered Saragossa and received its reluctant homage. The Aragonese reacted by forming a dynastic alliance with the Catalans and accepting the Count of Barcelona, Ramón Berenguer IV, as supreme ruler of Aragon. Thus came into existence the phenomenon of a 'Crown of Aragon', by which Catalonia and Aragon, though retaining their separate constitutions, recognized a common ruler. The ruling house was that of the counts of Barcelona, who after the death of Ramón Berenguer took on the title of king. The coexistence of Aragon and Catalonia was fruitful. The Catalans respected the customs and language of the Aragonese, and this exercise in liberal government was to prove useful when the time came to coexist with yet another kingdom, Valencia, which was added to the Crown a century later.

By the early thirteenth century the broad lines of peninsular history had been set. The Muslims remained confined to the kingdom of Granada: over two centuries were to pass before Castile, ruled after St Ferdinand by his militarily less capable son Alfonso the Wise (1252–84), could resume the Reconquest. It was a time for consolidation: Alfonso distinguished himself as the great codifier of Castilian law, in particular the code of Las Siete Partidas (1265). Castilian predominance was unmistakable. The kingdom embraced over half the land mass of the peninsula and the great majority of its inhabitants. Over most of its territories the language spoken was Castilian. In the Crown of Aragon the Catalans were the pace-setters. By settling the newly annexed Muslim-populated lands of Valencia, they made Valencia into a province that was (and has remained into recent times) overwhelmingly Catalan in race and language.

Though the aim of the Reconquest was to eliminate Arab power, it did not necessarily involve elimination of the Arab population. No state could have coped adequately with a sudden withdrawal of all Muslims from Spain. The slow progress of conquest therefore allowed Christian society to adapt to changing political conditions. In effect, the Christians 'colonized' those regions where they encountered a working peasantry. Royal grants gave them ownership of the southern estates controlled by Moors. They continued to exploit them with the help of the subjected Muslim peasants, who were treated virtually as serfs. Where there were few native peasants, Christians from the frontier lands came and settled the soil on a contractual basis with the new lords. Because of the moving frontier in Andalucia, the new Christian owners were less interested in domestic agriculture than in rearing sheep. In Valencia the frontier was more settled since there was no further scope for expansion. Here the agrarian economy of Christian landlords and Muslim (later, after conversion, called *morisco*) peasants continued profitably into the early seventeenth century.

In Castile the Crown relied heavily on an independent nobility for the defence of the frontiers. This leaf from a thirteenth-century collection of feudal donations depicts King Alfonso VIII of Castile and Queen Eleanor donating the town of Ucles to the monastic military order of Santiago.

In Aragon a more formal feudalism developed, in which the nobility depended on the monarch for its privileges. This miniature illustrates a feudal donation.

The warrior nobles of the Reconquest frontier were granted lands and privileges which their families have held down to today. The kings of Castile did not distribute such rewards only out of gratitude: it was obvious that the frontier could not be held save by giving the meritorious a secure investment in it. Even this could not prevent the ambitious few, like the Cid, striking out on their own, creating their own principalities and sometimes allying with the Moor against their own king. Out of the Reconquest there thus rose a mystique of the great noble. In Castile, where the feudal system of mutual obligations between lord and vassal never took hold, largely because of the fluid nature of landed and personal obligations in a society at permanent war, the noble became a minor king. In Aragon, which was more closely influenced by European legislation and social patterns, a formal feudalism tended to restrict ambitious nobles; it also created a class of depressed peasantry in Catalonia (the *payeses de remensa*) who took part in a great upsurge of revolt at the end of the fifteenth century. The class of military adventurers was always large in a society where constant war against the Moor was a norm. There arose a large sector of lesser nobles, the *hidalgos* (*hijos de algo*, sons of some substance, usually landed), whose feats gave the Reconquest its chivalric dimension. These were the Christian knights celebrated in the ballads or romances known in French as the *chansons de geste* and in Castilian as *cantares de gesta*: ballads such as the *Song of Roland* or the *Poem of the Cid*.

The movement and activity in Hispanic society of the Reconquest bred a remarkable amount of freedom. Just as the nobles were granted privileges for their hazardous role on the frontier, so the peasantry was encouraged to settle in formerly Muslim lands on favourable terms. Settlement charters granted to new frontier towns show the concession of numerous rights, all of which went to strengthen the acute pride in local privileges that marks the Spaniard. Concessions to citizens venturing to settle the uneasy frontier areas were generous. Municipalities which pressed hard enough were able to obtain a confirmation of their rights (*fueros*) from the Crown. Townships thus came to play a big part in resettlement, as they were later to do during the conquest of America. Smaller towns in Castile were allowed to become *behetrías*, that is, to choose their own lord at will. At the same time the frontier peasantry or shepherds, particularly in Castile, enjoyed not merely personal freedom (in contrast to the servitude in north-eastern Spain and over much of western Europe) but also communal privileges such as rights of pasture and rights to cut wood.

In these circumstances Reconquest Spain tended to breed an energetic, independent lower class at the same time as it was producing a highly privileged and propertied aristocracy. This somewhat democratic environment made the Hispanic kingdoms the first in Europe to produce significant representative institutions. By the late twelfth century the cities and towns of León and Aragon had begun to participate in representative assemblies; this does not seem to have occurred in Castile before the mid-thirteenth century. The *cortes* of the Hispanic realms thus preceded the existence of the first English Parliament by a full century. Spain's medieval constitutional heritage is an important aspect of peninsular history which is always worth bearing in mind when allegations are made about the authoritarian nature of Spanish political institutions.

While the peninsula was being recovered for Christianity, the Catalans had commenced a policy of expansion beyond it. Aragonese ambitions to cross the Pyrenees were of long standing. In the late twelfth century the authority of the Catalan counts extended from Béarn in the Pyrenees through Toulouse to Provence on the Mediterranean coast. This appeared to be the beginning of a large land empire, but a serious military reversal in 1213 put an end to further hopes of trans-Pyrenean sovereignty, and in 1258 James I of Aragon (1213-76), known as the Conqueror, signed away all these territories

Libre de cõsolat tractãt dels fets marítims zc.

to St Louis of France. The loss of the trans-Pyrenean territories was a blessing in disguise, for Aragon was now to divert its considerable energies towards the Mediterranean.

James I gave the first great impulse to eastern expansion by the conquest of Mallorca in 1229. By 1235 all the Balearic Islands had been annexed. One result was a quick growth in the maritime activity of Barcelona, and it was in this period that the famous Llibre del Consulat de Mar, Catalonia's first maritime code, was drawn up. The Crown of Aragon now became decidedly the most vigorous force in the peninsula, and the founder of the first Spanish overseas empire. James I's successor Peter the Great annexed Sicily in 1282; in 1327 Sardinia was finally conquered. In the early fourteenth century the crumbling Byzantine Empire called for help against the Turks. A Catalan army of eight thousand, called the 'Great Company of Catalans' and commanded by the German adventurer Roger de Flor, set sail from Sicily. In Greece they fought against the Turks, met Byzantine treachery ('Catalan vengeance' soon became proverbial), and established a Catalan duchy in Athens. Catalan became the official language in Thebes and Athens, and the Catalan adventurers,

Left, a thirteenth-century naval expedition sets sail: illustration from the *Cantigas de Santa Maria*, a collection of medieval poetry and music compiled by Alfonso X.

Right, title-page of the first printed edition of the *Llibre del Consulat de Mar*, published in 1502.

Abraham Cresque's world map, compiled for Peter III of Aragon in 1375, was a triumph of cartography, of benefit to sailors and scholars alike. *Above*, astronomical table and, *opposite*, two panels showing the Far East.

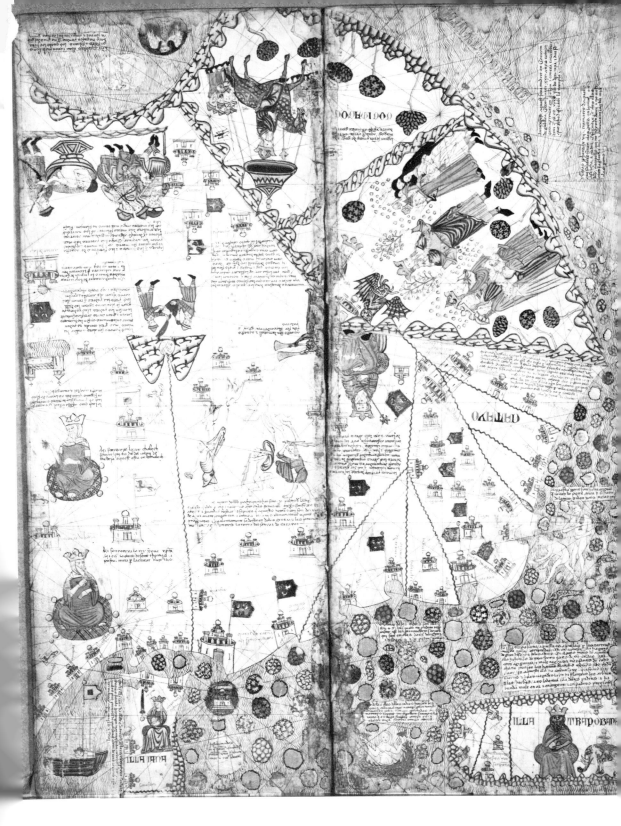

'sons of perdition, schooled in iniquity' as one irate pope called them, heard Mass in the Parthenon. It was one of the great moments of achievement in Catalan and Spanish history.

The vigour of Hispanic society at this epoch was reflected in its arts and letters. No longer isolated, literature came into touch with Christian Europe. Learning was promoted in the universities, of which the first was that of Palencia in 1212. Salamanca, the most eminent of the Castilian universities, was founded by St Ferdinand in 1242. The first Catalan creation was that of Lérida, in 1300. Of the early luminaries of this period the most distinguished was the Catalan philosopher, a native of Mallorca, Ramón Llull (d. 1315). Writing in Arabic, Catalan and Latin, Llull was simultaneously poet, philosopher and mystic, an outstanding product of the many complex strands in Hispanic civilization. In Castile the best known of the poets of the early fourteenth century was the Archpriest of Hita, whose

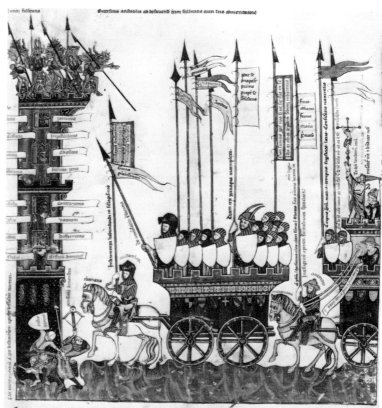

Illustration from a thirteenth-century biography of Ramón Llull showing Aristotle and his commentators, among them Averroes, marching to attack the tower of falsehood. It was through Arab writers such as Averroes that Aristotle's work was introduced into western Europe.

Book of True Love presents, like Chaucer, a both witty and serious picture of life in his day.

The fourteenth and fifteenth centuries, during which the Reconquest was in abeyance, saw greater tension among the Christian dynasties and an intensification of internal struggles. In the mid-fourteenth century Castile, ruled by Peter the Cruel (1350–69), an aptly named monarch, began a war against Aragon, then ruled by Peter the Ceremonious (1336–87), which lasted for fourteen years. At the same time Peter the Cruel had to conduct an internal war against dissident nobles led by his bastard half-brother Henry of Trastámara. These bitter conflicts for peninsular supremacy were made all the more serious by the reliance of both sides on foreign allies, participants in the European Hundred Years War. While the French supported Aragon, the English (captained by the Black Prince) tended to support Peter the Cruel. The wars ended with the capture of Peter and his death in 1369 at the hands of his half-brother Henry of Trastámara, who now became King of Castile as Henry II (1369–79). The House of Trastamara moved on to further successes when a major dispute over the succession to the Aragonese throne in the early fifteenth century was settled in 1412 by a papally inspired decision, the Sentence of Caspe, by which the Castilian Ferdinand of Antequera, a grandson of Henry II, was chosen as King of Aragon. In this way the Trastamaras came to rule over both Castile and Aragon until they were succeeded in both Crowns by the House of Habsburg. It was a hopeful step towards peninsular unity, though the immediate impact was small. Catalan interest was still directed towards the Mediterranean empire, which reached its zenith under Ferdinand's son Alfonso the Magnanimous (1416–58). It was Alfonso who finally secured the kingdom of Naples in the course of the fifteenth century and became overlord of Albania.

The Christian kingdoms modified their character in the course of expansion. As the centre of a seaborne empire, Barcelona grew to rival Genoa in the commerce of the western Mediterranean. Industrial growth in the province boosted the city's trade, and a prosperous, independent-minded élite of Catalans extended their trading interests abroad from the thirteenth century onwards. The life-blood of Aragon's Mediterranean empire was commerce. Sicily was a vital acquisition because it supplied grain to an under-producing Catalonia. The goods and dyes of the Levant added to the incoming trade. Commercial greatness contributed to the status of the Catalan-Aragonese bourgeoisie, who began to play a leading part in urban and political life. Simultaneously, the kings began to tame their nobility. Thus the Catalan-Aragonese aristocracy did not attain the political importance in Aragon that the Castilian nobles did in Castile.

Agricultural scenes from a fourteenth-century manuscript.

August: harvesting

October: the vintage

November: sowing

Right, shoe-making: detail from a fourteenth-century Catalan altarpiece.

Below, sheep-farming came to play an increasingly important part in the economy of medieval Spain: this capital from Gerona cathedral depicts Jacob watering his flock.

Opposite, the silk exchange at Valencia, built in the late fifteenth century as a centre for the city's expanding commercial activity.

Castile's strength had never been in its economy. Despite its immense land mass and its wide variety of produce, its population was largely engaged in localized subsistence production. Expansion added to its territory the dry, difficult surfaces of New Castile and Extremadura and the harsh terrain of Andalucia. Rather than eke out a living from the soil, many turned to sheep-farming. Privileges granted to the sheep-owners in the twelfth century by Alfonso X and Alfonso XI led to the formation of a powerful sheep-owners' guild, the Mesta, that was to play a major role in the Castilian economy. The flocks of sheep, with their guaranteed rights of grazing over the countryside, supplied the wool that became the mainstay of Castile's export trade.

One of the most unhappy results of the universal success of Christian arms was the breakdown of community relations in Spain. At times of peace it had been common for the two sides to visit each other, to trade and even to intermarry. When noble families intermarried it was not unknown for a Christian wife to give up her religion, with her family's consent, and embrace Islam. The Reconquest was never an exclusively ideological crusade. Frontiersmen had zeal for land, no less than religion, prominent in their minds. The example of the Cid shows clearly that loyalties could be changed without prejudice. The historian of Arab Spain, Reinhard Dozy, has argued that 'a Spanish

knight of the Middle Ages fought neither for his country nor for his religion; he fought, like the Cid, to get something to eat, whether under a Christian or a Muslim prince.' A thirteenth-century Castilian writer observed that 'there is war between the Christians and the Moors, and there will be, until the Christians have got back the lands which the Moors took from them by force; for neither because of the law [i.e. faith] nor because of the sect that they hold to, would there be war between them.' Christians, Muslims and Jews felt that they were all obliged to coexist, a feeling which was common even at the height of the Reconquest, when it was possible for Ramón Llull to compose a dialogue in Arabic in which the three characters were a Christian, a Moor and a Jew. St Ferdinand of Castile, himself the most successful of Reconquest kings, adopted the title 'King of the Three Religions'.

This basically tolerant attitude, born of the necessity to coexist within the same land, vanished in the wake of the Almoravids, the Almohads and the reconquering Christians.

The Muslims of Al-Andalus had to readjust to the realities of Christian rule. Those who continued under Christian domination were known as *mudéjares*, and were allowed their own religion and customs just as the Mozarabs under Islamic rule had been allowed theirs. It was through the Mudejars that Muslim culture triumphed

Thirteenth-century 'strip cartoons' depicting the conversion of Jews, *top*, and Moors. In each case the image of the Virgin Mary has brought about a miraculous transformation.

over the Christian world in the very throes of political and military defeat. After its capture by the Christians, Toledo immediately became the intellectual capital of Castile, because of the transmission of Muslim and Jewish learning. The School of Translators of Toledo in the twelfth and thirteenth centuries rendered into Latin the great Semitic treatises on philosophy, medicine, mathematics, alchemy. Names such as Avicenna (Ibn-Sina), Al-Ghazali and Ibn-Masarra became known to European readers. At the same time the works of Averroes and Maimonides filtered through to Christian scholars. But it was principally in art that the Mudejars transmitted Muslim culture for the greater visual delight of posterity. The supreme example of fourteenth-century Mudejar craftsmanship is the Alcázar or royal palace built for himself in Seville by Peter the Cruel in about 1364. Totally Moorish in construction and decoration, it is vivid evidence of the acceptance by Castilians of what they most admired in Islamic civilization. The construction a century later at Coca (Segovia) of a castle for the Fonseca family in a purely Mudejar style underlines the continued popularity of the Moorish style. But the Mudejar people were treated with contempt. The urban population had their rights closely restricted by legislation, and the rural population were exploited and depressed until they revolted (as in 1263 in Andalucia), which led to their expulsion from the country.

It was the smaller Jewish minority that suffered the worst. The earliest persecutions had been under the Visigoths, particularly after their conversion to Catholicism. Ferocious laws reduced them literally to slavery. Under Muslim rule the Jews had fared better, and they even helped the Arabs against their Visigothic oppressors. As 'people of the book', with no territorial ambitions like the Christians, the Jews were usually tolerated in the Muslim kingdoms and became valuable urban artisans and traders. Jewish culture (the language used was Arabic) flourished in Al-Andalus. It was significant that the scholarship of a Maimonides was nurtured in Córdoba rather than in the Christian north.

When Toledo fell to the Christians the Jews, whose chief city it had always been, added their talents to promote Latin culture, and became key members of the School of Translators. Both in Aragon and Castile valuable financial aid had been rendered to the kings by Jews: in the fourteenth century Alfonso III of Aragon claimed that 'our predecessors have tolerated and suffered the Jews in their territories because these Jews are the strong-box and treasury of the kings.' They were also prominent in many professions and in trade, and had a virtual monopoly of medical practice. The thirteenth century was the last great period during which Jews enjoyed some measure of community freedom. Rulers like Alfonso X of Castile and James I of

Opposite, the Alcázar at Coca, near Segovia, built by Moorish architects in about 1400 for the Archbishop of Seville.

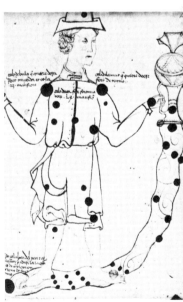

Above, Leo and Aquarius, two illustrations from mid-fourteenth-century astronomical tables.

49

Mostra cona so figurada en la uerga de aaron.

Jr moyses â la uga de aaron en lo tabernacle puntut de du sens humor de tra flore e feu fuytes e fruyt.

ad oriente e era clausa. e dixit dns ad me. Porta hec clausa erit et non aperiet. et uir non transibit p cam. qm dns deus ursl ingssus est per eam.

Que ma dona deguesses e tan uerge en figura de le so monstrat a ezechiel propheta en la p...ma ...lun capitol.

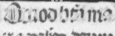

Co meu en cos m...r... erten.

Jeronimus

E duxit me ma de...t domū pax te me... e... som ezechu li t... a... cap ...at ezechiel e contra me ad uiā porte sciuary e tio ns q respiciebat

Ezechiel vio gue a la uia dla porta del sciuary de fores q regarda uers orient e era closa. e dix me senyor amj. Aqsta porta sera closa e hō no passara pella. car nie seyor deus de ursl es passat pella. Co meu en cos que no erten la figura.

Aragon continued to award them substantial favours, but the Christian victories altered permanently the relationship between the three great religious groupings. Popular and clerical hostility was aggravated during periods of economic depression and epidemics. Several members of the Jewish élite converted to Christianity and continued to hold high office as bishops of the Church or ministers of state. But the mass of the community suffered increasingly during the fourteenth century from pogroms, the most devastating and widespread of which took place in 1391. Mass conversion forced on Jews in 1391 swelled the ranks of the often insincere Semitic converts, known as *conversos* or 'New Christians'.

The anti-Semitic outrages of the late fourteenth century occurred in both Castile and Aragon, a sign of the common problems they shared. In the fifteenth century both realms had to face other joint problems. In Castile the great magnates aspired to protect their gains against the Crown and so plunged the realm into civil war. In Catalonia, where the nobles were weaker, it was the peasantry and urban classes that gave expression to their unrest. This turbulence was not as disruptive of peninsular unity as in previous centuries, largely because of the common dynasty ruling over both states. Cultural interchange also became common, writers in Aragon for example often producing their works indifferently in either Catalan or Castilian.

By the end of the fifteenth century the long decades of revolt and civil war in the two kingdoms had produced a yearning for peace. The disputes under Henry IV of Castile (1454–74), the Impotent, centred round the legitimacy of his daughter and heir Juana. Opponents of Juana supported the rights of the King's sister Isabella, who in 1469 had married Ferdinand, heir to the throne of Aragon. The ensuing civil war in Castile was settled in Isabella's favour by 1479. Ferdinand and Isabella thereafter ruled both realms jointly: the era of dynastic conflicts had come to an end, a new epoch began. The Reconquest outlook of Castile and the expansionist vigour of Catalonia merged into a common national policy.

The reign of Ferdinand and Isabella marks the beginning of Spain's modern history. In the years they ruled (Isabella died in 1504, Ferdinand in 1516) the habit of obedience to the Crown was firmly inculcated. Spain – we shall use the term in its modern sense of the Iberian peninsula without Portugal – remained little more than an aspiration, and unity was still very distant; but the active co-operation of its two principal kingdoms laid a secure basis for its achievements. At the same time it was clear that the spirit of the new Spain was to be that of its strongest constituent, Castile: a nation fired less by the commercial enterprise that had created the Catalan Empire than by the proud military and crusading spirit that had inspired the Reconquest.

Despite important positions in the professions and trade the Jewish community could never feel entirely secure. *Opposite*, leaf from a fourteenth-century Catalan manuscript showing the Devil blinding a Jew; the surrounding text is of passages from the Old Testament that the Jews, blind to the truth, had failed to understand. *Below*, a Jew wearing the distinctive yellow circle that was the badge of his race: detail from a fourteenth-century Catalan wall-painting.

In order to complete the Reconquest the united Christian king-doms turned their attention to Granada. Throughout the 1480s Arab towns fell before the slow and painful advance. Ronda was taken in 1485, Málaga in 1487. Finally Granada, under its last king, Boabdil, capitulated after a year and a half of sieges. In January 1492 Ferdinand and Isabella entered the Alhambra, last and most beautiful of the Moorish palaces in the peninsula. The terms of surrender, which included tolerance of Islam, were respected for a few years and then openly breached. When the Granadans rebelled in 1501 they were ordered to convert or suffer expulsion. The Moors were the last great minority to suffer in this way. Ten years previously, in 1492, the Jews had been given the same choice.

The action of the Catholic Monarchs ('Los Reyes Católicos', a title granted to them by the Pope) have traditionally been explained as a move to unify the peninsula in faith. Some modern political movements have looked to the Catholic Monarchs as the forerunners of their own wish to give the nation a rigid conservative ideology. Any account of the policies of Ferdinand and Isabella consequently tends to have contemporary relevance. The fact is that there does not appear to have been any single-minded drive towards unity, either in politics or in religion. The conquest of Granada and the expulsion of the Jews were mainly completions of a long historical development.

Castile and Aragon came together in the persons of their rulers, but were otherwise wholly separate, and no attempt was made to unite them. Each kingdom kept its own institutions jealously. The monarchs nevertheless acted as one ruler wherever possible. So in-sistent was Isabella on having all their activities recorded as joint

Friar preaching to a group of Moors: title-page from Ricol-dus' *Improbatio Alcorani* (*Dis-proving the Koran*), published in 1500.

On the fall of Granada in 1492 Christianity finally triumphed in Spain. These two reliefs from Granada cathedral illustrate the surrender of the city, and, *left*, the forced baptism of Moorish women.

53

ones that a court chronicler satirized her attitude by pretending to report that 'on such and such a day, the king and queen gave birth to a daughter'. The policies they pursued were distinct in each kingdom. Aragon, with its federal structure, its three separate parliaments (of Aragon, Catalonia and Valencia) and its local *fueros*, enjoyed a degree of autonomy that set a limit on the King's powers. In Castile, on the other hand, the constitutional tradition had never been strong, and the Crown therefore enjoyed very extensive powers. Much that was new in the domestic policy of the Catholic Monarchs was consequently practised in Castile, urgently in need of reconstruction after the ruinous civil wars.

The internal consolidation of Castile was carried through by an inevitable mixture of force and compromise. Isabella travelled throughout her realms, intent on restoring order: dissident nobles were arrested, their castles razed, their property confiscated. 'She was much inclined to do justice,' says one chronicler, 'so much so that it was said of her that she followed more the path of sternness than of compassion.' But no monarch could afford to alienate her own ruling class. Isabella subdued the dissident, but rewarded the faithful to an extent that consolidated their hold on the state and economy of Castile for centuries. Her most famous measures were designed to secure the position of the Crown. Pacification of the countryside was put into the hands of brotherhoods (*hermandades*) of local police; the nobles were forbidden to make private war; the three great military orders were made subordinate to the Crown and their masterships invested in the monarch. In 1480 grants of lands made by the Crown to the nobles without sufficient cause were revoked. But the few lands lost by the nobles in 1480 were more than compensated for by the lands which they acquired through the conquest of Granada, when the greater part of the kingdom was given to the aristocracy. Moreover, they retained all their normal privileges, such as immunity from taxation, torture and imprisonment for debt. At the same time they were assigned the chief places in the new councils of state that the Crown instituted in order to centralize the administrative and financial system.

Administrative reforms supplied Castile with the basic machinery it was to use during its career as a world power. Closer control over the state both at the centre and in the municipalities (where Ferdinand and Isabella instituted the post of *corregidor* or civil governor) created a well-knit political structure which Castilians, after decades of civil disruption, appear to have accepted willingly. In the process, there was some loss of constitutional liberty, and Castile never approached the level of parliamentary government that existed in Aragon.

In Aragon Ferdinand had approached his problems in a more constitutional way. The Sentence of Guadalupe in 1486 offered a compromise solution to the difficult peasant question in Catalonia. The municipalities were assured a degree of autonomy. The rights of the *cortes* were confirmed. In Catalonia the King remained essentially what he had been in medieval times: a supreme lord, but with strict limits on his power. No laws, for example, could be altered without the consent of the *cortes*. Whereas in Castile the Crown was in a position to exercise absolute power, in Catalonia (and throughout Aragon) it was limited by the traditional contractual relationship. This contrast was to be profoundly important for the later history of the two Crowns, and lay at the root of the major 'rebellions' – in 1591, 1640, 1705 – that the Aragonese were subsequently to undertake against Castile. The contrast likewise meant that it was the Crown of Castile that was responsible for the more arbitrary actions associated with the government of 'Spain'.

The harsher methods of Castile can be seen most clearly in the later history of the Jews. Though anti-Semitism was universal in the peninsula, as the pogroms of 1391 proved, its institutionalization occurred only in Castile. Rivalry and resentment at the success of the *conversos* and Jews intensified popular anti-Semitism. Throughout southern Castile, argued a polemic of 1488, of all the *conversos* 'hardly

Ferdinand and Isabella, the Catholic Monarchs; they brought religious unity to Spain and began to build a New World empire. This detail from a tapestry in Lérida cathedral shows them enthroned, surrounded by members of their court.

One of the most powerful instruments of religious and political orthodoxy ever devised, the Inquisition sent over two thousand *conversos* to the stake during the 1480s: detail from *Auto de Fe*, attributed to Pedro Berruguete.

any are true Christians, as is well known in all Spain'. Pressure on Isabella led to the foundation in 1478 of the Spanish Inquisition, over which the Crown was given almost full control by the Pope. Aragon had its own Inquisition, of medieval origin, but the new Castilian Inquisition was introduced there on Ferdinand's orders, despite bitter and prolonged opposition from the public authorities. When the first Inquisitor-General, Tomás de Torquemada, was appointed, he exercised jurisdiction over both Castile and Aragon, and so became the only person in Spain whose writ ran unimpeded over both realms.

The Inquisition was founded to solve one specific problem: the religious and public status of *conversos*. Unbaptized Jews were not subject to its jurisdiction. The early proceedings were undoubtedly bloody: a contemporary historian estimated that in Seville alone between 1480 and 1488 the tribunal had burnt over seven hundred people and punished several thousands. A later historian, the Jesuit Juan de Mariana, admitted that some aspects of the Inquisition 'appeared very oppressive to Spaniards'. But because the tribunal was a tool of deep-seated prejudices, those who directed it were able to bring into being a terrifying social weapon that helped to mould the thinking of Spaniards for centuries. It was one of the most powerful forces in the everyday life of sixteenth- and seventeenth-century Spain. Because there were few or no Protestants for it to deal with, it was much less concerned with heresy than is usually thought. *Conversos* accused of practising the Jewish faith were its main line of business, but such cases tended to occur only at specific periods and often had political rather than religious overtones. Where neither Protestants nor Jews existed the Inquisition still intruded regularly into daily life, as the self-appointed guardian of orthodoxy and morality, with extensive powers to prosecute subversive or disrespectful words, thoughts and writings; sexual misbehaviour; bigamy; usury; superstitious practices; and other crimes large or small. Gradually the nation learned to identify the Inquisition with the Catholic faith, an identification which was quite widely accepted in Spain in the sixteenth century but which by the eighteenth century led, as a chief minister of the Crown commented, to the growth of 'hatred not merely of the Inquisition but of religion itself'. The tribunal set itself a task which was more recognizably racialist than religious: to purify peninsular Catholicism by eliminating from the Church and its clergy all descendants of Jewish or Moorish blood. The task was carried out with an efficiency that has left a permanent mark on Spanish history. Even in modern times distrust of Jews and Arabs has played a significant role in Spanish politics.

The positive achievement of the Inquisition, in providing Spain with a national ideology, must be set against the imbalance this introduced. The imposition of conformity on the nation in the course of the sixteenth century meant a sacrifice of much of the cultural promise of the reign of Ferdinand and Isabella.

The activities of the Inquisition against *conversos* were accompanied by a systematic campaign against unconverted Jews. The Catholic Monarchs approved legislation to make them wear distinctive badges (a common medieval practice), and sanctioned expulsions of Jews from particular areas. Jewish gold had contributed handsomely to the campaign that ended in the surrender of Granada. Once the city had fallen, however, it was decided to rid Spain completely of Jews, and in March 1492 an edict offering them a choice between conversion and expulsion was issued. It is estimated that over 165,000 emigrated. Probably at least 50,000 stayed behind and chose conversion. The consequences of the expulsion are difficult to assess. The Sultan of Turkey is said to have remarked at a later date that he 'marvelled greatly at expelling the Jews from Spain, since this was to expel its wealth'. The attack on *conversos* and Jews certainly struck at the country's economy. But Isabella, as her secretary reported, 'set little importance on the decline in her revenue, and prized highly the purity

of her lands'. In the long run, the elimination of the Jews prejudiced the evolution of a capitalist middle class and thereby hindered the economic future of Spain. The tactic of expelling an uncomfortable but productive racial minority was one that Castile would repeat in the early seventeenth century. This disdain for wealth was one of the characteristics of the Reconquest code of Castilians. As a fifteenth-century bishop of Burgos put it when addressing a meeting abroad: 'Spaniards do not prize great wealth, but rather, virtue; nor do they measure a man's honour by the store of his money but by the quality of his beautiful deeds.'

The vigorous, warlike society of fifteenth-century Castile was the stage for a great flowering of literature in all its forms. Foreign influences from France and Italy played an important part in refining and perfecting style. The early century produced work from members of the aristocratic, literary élite like the Marquis of Santillana (d. 1458) and Jorge Manrique (d. 1479). Their output was paralleled on the other side of Spain by that of the Valencian poet Auzias March (d. 1459). At the same time, the chivalric ideals of the Reconquest were translated into popular literature of knight-errantry in the form of two prose works which had a great success in their day. One of these, *Tirant lo Blanch* (1460), was written in Catalan; the other, *Amadis de Gaula* (1508), in Castilian. Perhaps the best known of the prose works of this time was the *Celestina*, a tragi-comedy written by the *converso* Fernando de Rojas and published in 1499.

The *Celestina* was produced under the Catholic Monarchs, and is testimony to the cultural renaissance then dawning in Spain. New influences were brought by scholars from Italy. The great Andalucian scholar Antonio de Nebrija went to Bologna and returned as the chief ornament of the new university of Alcalá, founded in 1508 by the Archbishop of Toledo, Cardinal Cisneros. It was at Alcalá that one of the wonders of the age was prepared: a great Polygot Bible drawn up under the auspices of Cisneros, with the Hebrew, Aramaic and Greek originals printed in columns parallel to the Latin. The Valencian school produced at this period its greatest writer – the philosopher Juan Luis Vives (d. 1540), who was to become a permanent exile from his native land becuase of his Jewish blood. The fate of Vives foreshadowed that of other disciples of Renaissance humanism. The early intellectual promise of the reign, its sympathy with the outlook of the great Dutch scholar Erasmus, was crushed by the Inquisition.

The internal ordering of Spain was outmatched by developments abroad. One event of the year 1492 is unforgettable. That autumn Christopher Columbus, with three small ships, made his first landfall on American soil, in the Bahamas. Taken in conjunction with the fall of Granada that spring and the expulsion of the Jews later in the

Cardinal Cisneros (1436–1517), who embodied that mixture of militant Christianity and learned humanism characteristic of sixteenth-century Spain. Zealous for mass conversion of the Moors, he also founded the university of Alcalá and encouraged the completion of the Polyglot Bible (begun in 1502).

Woodcut from the title-page of the 1526 edition of *Celestina*, Fernando de Rojas' tragi-comic tale of seduction and disaster.

summer, the discovery of America made 1492 the most remarkable year in Spanish history.

It is difficult to explain why empires grow, and the Spanish Empire is no exception. Castile was a relatively poor country, with neither industry nor agriculture enough to make it wealthy (under Isabella the import of wheat for domestic needs became habitual). Aragon by the fifteenth century was economically in decline. Yet it was at this in-auspicious juncture that the two realms embarked on a period of empire-building. Internal peace freed the chivalry of Spain for ex-ternal adventures. After 1495 Ferdinand pursued the traditional interests of Catalonia in Italian territory, but the troops he used there against the French were led by a Castilian general, Gonsalvo de Córdoba, 'the great captain', fresh from the wars of Granada. Ferdinand's foreign policy brought the two Crowns directly into European politics, and the annexation of the kingdom of Naples in 1504 began Spanish domination of Italy and the western Mediter-ranean. In 1512 the conquest of Navarre completed the unification of all peninsular territory outside Portugal.

The expansion of Castile into America proved to be the most remarkable of the factors that gave Castile leadership of the destinies of Spain. The first and vital step to the Indies was possession of the Canary Islands, the 'Fortunate Isles' which classical writers located beyond the explored edge of the world. They were formally ceded to Castile by Portugal in 1477. The next stage was the discovery of the new lands to the west by Columbus, and the colonization of the West

Indies in the subsequent twenty years. Not until Cortes's expedition to Mexico in 1519 did the Spaniards become aware of the immense riches of the New World, and of the high degree of civilization that already existed there. After the fall of the Aztec capital to Cortes, adventurers swarmed into the mainland and within a generation had utterly changed the history of America.

The 'Indies', as the Americas were commonly called in Spanish, were the exclusive possession of Castile, since Columbus had received his commission from Isabella only. All Aragonese were in theory excluded from the New World. The administration and language introduced there were both Castilian. Inheritance of so vast a continent evoked an enthusiastic response from Castilians, who thereafter dominated every stage of growth of the world-wide empire of Spain. The men who flocked to America reflected both the best and the worst of Reconquest Castile: the worst, in their brutality and greed for wealth, traits common both to Cortés, the gentlemanly conqueror

The .Virgin of Christopher Columbus, anonymous sixteenth-century painting.

of Mexico, and Pizarro, the illiterate conqueror of Peru; the best, in their missionary zeal, the selfless evangelizing work of the early Franciscans, the passion for justice of the Dominican friar Las Casas. The crimes of Spain in America were many, ranging from Indian massacres to the introduction of black slavery. But against this there was a constant anxiety, unknown in more recent empires, to see justice done, to abide by the law of nations, and to allow a wide margin of dissent. Nowhere else but in this empire could the King (it was Charles V, in 1550) have expressly suspended all further conquests until a debate had been held between two theologians about the justice of Spain's position in the Indies.

The achievement of the reign of Ferdinand and Isabella was immense. But an important part in it must be attributed to Cardinal Cisneros. He it was who furthered the work of the Inquisition, advanced learning and culture, and gave the first successful impulse to Spanish imperialism by the capture of the North African fort of Oran in 1509, in a campaign that he led in person. By his reforms of the Spanish Church, moreover, Cisneros carried out an institutional reformation that predated the Protestant one in Europe. When Ferdinand died in 1516 Spain was still only on the threshold of status as a world power, but already the most characteristic features of its modern history – its social and religious conservatism, its imperialist ambitions, its artistic and literary promise – had been fixed. Writers of the following century were in no doubt that the reign of the Catholic Monarchs represented the pinnacle of Spanish achievement. It had been the true golden age of Spain's history. 'That was a golden time and a time of justice', claimed the contemporary historian Fernández de Oviedo, looking back on Isabella's reign. 'Who cannot see', wrote one of the greatest humanists of the reign, Nebrija, 'that although the title of Empire is in Germany, its reality lies in the power of the Spanish monarchs who, masters of a large part of Italy and the isles of the Mediterranean Sea, carry the war to Africa, and send out their fleet, following the course of the stars, to the isles of the Indies and the New World, linking the Orient to the western boundary of Spain and Africa.'

Ferdinand and Isabella as emperors of the world in a late fifteenth-century Flemish tapestry, *opposite.*

The Cross is brought to the three continents: printer's device from a historical account of the reign of Ferdinand and Isabella published in 1578.

SVI · IPSIVS
TRIVMPHATORI

3

The Habsburg Centuries

The two centuries during which the House of Habsburg ruled Spain saw the rise and decay of Spanish world supremacy. As so often before, what transpired was the result of dynastic accident. The daughter of Ferdinand and Isabella, Juana, married into the House of Habsburg, and her son, Charles of Burgundy, was brought up in the Netherlands. Juana became Queen of Castile on her mother's death in 1504, but she was soon reckoned to be mentally incapable of ruling, and Ferdinand was recognized as heir to the throne. In 1516 Ferdinand died, after naming Charles as his heir. Charles then became King of both Castile and Aragon. Within a couple of years he succeeded his other grandfather as Holy Roman Emperor. By 1519, at the age of nineteen, Charles (the First in Castile, but the fifth emperor of that name) held in his hands the Empire and its dependencies, the Netherlands, and Spain with its world-wide empire. He was now the most powerful monarch in the world. Spaniards never reconciled themselves fully to participation in this universal monarchy, feeling that their own peninsular interests would be subordinated to foreign ones. The early years of their new King justified these fears.

Charles, with his heavy, square jaw and mouth that tended to hang open, looked unprepossessing: worse, he spoke no Castilian. But what most upset Castilians was his entourage, composed largely of Burgundians who very soon occupied the chief posts in his realm. The King had arrived in the peninsula in 1517. Within three years burning indignation at foreign exploitation led to the outbreak of a major rebellion in the chief cities of Castile. The revolt of the townships or *comuneros* opened in May 1520. In Valencia parallel uprisings known as *germanías* (brotherhoods) took place. But the victory of royalist forces at the Battle of Villalar a year later muted all further resistance to the new dynasty. This was the last serious civil dissidence to occur in Castile for nearly two centuries. Despite initial reluctance, Castilians and Spaniards soon came to identify themselves proudly with the imperial commitments of Charles V and his successors.

Thanks to Spain's new destiny, the services of the intrepid Castilian soldier were called upon for duty throughout Europe, and well beyond European frontiers as well. When in 1519 the vision of Aztec Mexico burst upon the eyes of Cortés and his men, one soldier who was present

Charles V, ruler of much of Europe and the Americas. This panel, from a series of tapestries representing the emperor's life, depicts him at his abdication, when he laid down the symbols of royalty and retired to a monastery near Madrid.

NETHERLANDS
LUXEMBURG
CHAROLAIS
BURGUNDY
MILAN
BALEARIC
IS.
SARDINIA
NAPLES
SICILY

CUBA

MEXICO

VENEZUELA

PERU

CHILE
RIO DE LA PLATA

PHILIPPINES
Manila

Map showing the extent of the Spanish Empire in the sixteenth century.

confided later in his memoirs that the sight had stunned them, even though 'some of us had been in many parts of the world, in Constantinople, in Rome, and all over Italy'. Spaniards were employed in increasing numbers in the Emperor's service, so tying them more closely to the idea of a universal monarchy. Charles himself was largely an absentee king, spending no more than sixteen years of his forty-year reign within the peninsula. That did not prevent him relying ever more heavily on the Spanish exchequer to pay (mainly with American bullion) for his expenses in the Empire. He also entertained considerable affection for Spain. A native French-speaker, he taught himself Castilian and in his later years would speak no other language. On one famous occasion in 1536, when speaking in Castilian to an assembly of prelates in the Vatican, he was interrupted by a French

AFRICAE
SVBINGATORI

Charles V as Conqueror of
Africa. The Emperor's African expeditions – he captured
Tunis in 1535, though he
failed at Algiers six years later
– brought him great popu-
larity among his Spanish subjects.

Below, the arms of the Emperor
Charles V: detail from a
Flemish tapestry.

bishop who could not understand him. 'Do not expect', the Emperor retorted, 'to hear from me any language but Spanish, which is so noble that it deserves to be known and understood by all Christian peoples.' When he retired from his imperial commitments and resigned his various charges, the imperial crown to his brother Ferdinand, the crown of Spain and the Netherlands to his son Philip, it was to Spain that he went. He died in 1558 in his haven near the monastery of Yuste in Extremadura.

The course to which Charles had committed Spain was a dazzling one. The 'imperial idea' was not one that ever played a part in the philosophy of the Catholic Monarchs. To that extent the Habsburgs were charting a new path for Spain: defence of the Faith against heresy, and the preservation of Europe from the Turk. But in most respects the political evolution of the country was a continuation of previous policy. The Emperor's absences made it impossible for fundamental innovation to take place in government. The highly efficient administrators, such as Los Cobos, who ran the state while Charles was in Germany, were carrying out no more than a holding operation. They restricted themselves to consolidating Crown authority, strengthening the bureaucracy, and ensuring an unimpeded flow of financial subsidies. Though Charles was the first monarch ever to rule over both Castile and Aragon, no progress was made under him to a closer relationship between the kingdoms. The failure to unify was accompanied by an inordinate emphasis on the leading position of Castile in the affairs of the monarchy.

The ordinary Castilian remained probably less aware of his country's European role than of what it was achieving in the New World. The American experience was slow to mature, but eventually it had a major impact on early sixteenth-century Spain. Through Seville, 'the new Babylon', the footloose soldiers, greedy adventurers and social rejects of the peninsula poured in their hundreds on to the ships bound for the West Indies. After the 1520s, when the mainland was opened up and Mexico with its wealth had fallen to Cortés, the urge to discover became overwhelming. A decade later, when Peru and its fabulous riches had been seized by Pizarro, it was uncontrollable. The conquistadors pressed northwards into the modern United States, in search of the legendary Seven Cities of Gold, the Fountain of Youth or the Isle of the Amazons; southwards into modern Venezuela in search of El Dorado. When surveying the tragic consequences for America of the Spanish invasion, it is worth bearing in mind that this was Europe's first great venture overseas, and that the errors, like the achievements, were inevitably on an heroic scale. Almost unintentionally, Spain achieved the destruction of America's finest civilizations, annihilated the greater part of the native population

Statue of a Spanish halberdier decorating a *conquistador* palace built in 1549 in Yucatan province, Mexico.

Opposite, sixteenth-century wood panel representing Cortes's expedition through Mexico.

68

Opposite, title-page of Antonio de Herrera's *Deeds of the Castilians* (1601). The compartments show incidents during the voyages of Columbus; the portraits are of Ferdinand, Isabella, Christopher Columbus and his brother Bartholomew.

Left, illustration from the German edition of *The Destruction of the Indies*, one of the many tracts Las Casas wrote against the conquest and forcible conversion of the Indies.

Below, traditional Inca customs intermingle with Spanish-Christian rites in this procession, held in Cuzco in about 1660 to celebrate the feast of Corpus Christi.

and implanted a new culture, one in many ways more savage than those it replaced. Yet it was the American experience which also brought out the amazing ability of the Spanish to penetrate, as one contemporary put it, 'through such rugged lands, such dense forests, such great mountains and deserts, and over such broad rivers'. Pizarro, with only 37 horses and 180 men, overthrew one of the world's greatest empires in Peru: feats of this order stagger the imagination. America also witnessed heroic efforts to right the errors of Spain, in the struggle of Las Casas for justice towards the Indians, and the lifetime of service given to the Negro slaves by the Catalan Jesuit Peter Claver.

Spain's dominion extended farther than the New World. By the late sixteenth century the Philippines had been annexed. From both Pacific and Atlantic coasts new wealth poured back into Spain. The rest of Europe looked on enviously. First treasure (from Mexico and Peru), then precious metals (principally silver from the mines of northern Mexico and central Bolivia) boosted royal finances. Other produce, such as leather and dyes, was highly profitable; but it was the bullion that attracted to Seville in the early sixteenth century the chief financiers of western Europe. Spain itself now became an El Dorado. Charles V had already begun to rely heavily on the peninsula for money (in 1540 he wrote, 'I cannot be sustained except by my kingdoms of Spain'), and it was in pursuit of imperial debts to them that the European banking houses, led by the Augsburg firm of Fugger, opened branches in Spain. The sudden wealth from America was diverted to meet the needs of foreign policy.

The political machinery of Spain during the Habsburg centuries has frequently, but misleadingly, been described as absolutist. Great efforts were certainly made to centralize administration, and constitutional checks on the Crown in Castile were few. But Habsburg centralism had no philosophy of unchecked royal power behind it. Many political theorists, like the Jesuit Mariana, believed that the king's authority derived from the people. Spanish kings might take arbitrary measures in their foreign dependencies, but within the peninsula their rule was usually circumspect, in Castile because of the need to placate the aristocracy, in Aragon because of the jealously guarded privileges of the towns and the *cortes*. Royal centralism existed principally in Castile, where it thrived at the expense of parliamentary government. It was practised in its most extreme form in America, which was governed directly from Madrid by the Council of the Indies, the sole body empowered to pass any legislation. All the chief administrative organs of Spain were dominated by Castilians. Castilians held the principal viceroyalties in Italy and America. Most significant of all, Castilian became the official language of Spain and of Latin America. Not without reason had Nebrija, when presenting a copy of his Castilian grammar to Queen Isabella, observed that 'language is always the companion of empire'.

The defeat of the municipalities after the revolt of the *comuneros* augured the decay of urban liberties in Castile. The *cortes*, consisting in practice of representatives of the nobility and selected townships, were summoned under Charles V primarily to grant taxes. Under Philip II they were called infrequently; during the reign of the last Habsburg, Charles II, they were not called at all. It did not follow from this that the power of the Crown had increased. Rather, the Habsburgs allowed the upper nobility to assume direction of the state. Charles V instituted the rank of 'grandee'. There were twenty-five in 1520; by the reign of Philip IV there were one hundred. The ruling councils of state were staffed by nobles, who exercised sway over the army, bureaucracy and social life. The pattern of landholding established by the Reconquest, when lands were granted to nobles in return for their services, developed into a situation in which by the seventeenth century the vast majority of the cities and landed estates of Spain were under aristocratic control.

The aggressive racial policies of this age were principally Castilian in inspiration. Active persecution of the Jewish and Moorish minorities, even after they had become Christian as *conversos* and *moriscos* respectively, was the accepted policy of both state and Inquisition. The process of eliminating the Moorish remnant from Spain was completed within about a century. Cisneros's persecution of the Granada Muslims was followed in 1502 by the formal prohibition of Islam in Granada. Under Charles V the *germanía* rebels in the Crown of Aragon forced the Muslims to convert to Christianity. But even as a subject and converted race the *moriscos* were not welcome. A great rebellion in the kingdom of Granada in 1570 led to suppression and expulsions. Finally in 1609 the Castilian government decided (despite the protests of the landlords of Valencia, who stood to lose their labour force) to expel from both Aragon and Castile virtually the entire body of *moriscos*, some 375,000 in all. The action was condemned by Cardinal Richelieu of France as 'the most barbarous stroke in human annals'. The over-all economic loss caused by the expulsion seems to have been small, except in Valencia, where the *moriscos* had been the mainstay of agriculture.

Spain's rise to world power was accompanied by a broadening of its cultural horizons. The Renaissance promise of the Catholic Monarchs continued to flourish. Under the early Habsburgs the last great Gothic cathedrals of Spain were erected, notably those of Segovia and Salamanca. Granada cathedral, constructed at this time, marks the move to the more ornamental style called 'plateresque'. Money was invested by both Crown and nobility in building imposing new

The great buildings of the early sixteenth century reflect the national confidence of Spain under the Habsburgs.

Above, interior view of Segovia cathedral (begun in 1522), masterpiece of late Gothic architecture, and the Case de la Conchas in Salamanca, so called because of the pilgrims' scallop-shells worked in relief on the façade.

Two examples of the ornate style of Renaissance building. *Right*, finely worked staircase of the Santa Cruz hospital, Toledo (erected between 1514 and 1544). *Opposite*, principal façade of the university of Salamanca (early sixteenth century). At the top, the Pope is shown issuing privileges; beneath him, the arms and imperial eagle of Charles V, and, at the bottom, portraits of Ferdinand and Isabella.

74

edifices – palaces, hospitals and churches. The literary arts were likewise full of promise. 'This our Spain,' a sixteenth-century writer was to claim, 'once considered crude and barbarous in the use of language, today exceeds the most flourishing culture of the Greeks and Latins.' But the development of Spanish genius underwent a severe change under Charles V. In his early years as King the most favoured cultural influence was Erasmus, courted alike by Cisneros and by the Inquisitor-General. Charles V assured him in 1527 that 'we shall always hold your honour and repute in the greatest esteem'. But with the Reformation suspicion fell on Erasmian humanism, and very soon his works were appearing on the Inquisition's Index of forbidden books. The liberal humanists began to be persecuted and hounded out of the country. Some, like Luis Vives, left for racial reasons.

The years bridging the reigns of Charles V (1516–56) and Philip II saw the rise of the religious problem. Protestantism in Spain was virtually still-born. It had no more than a handful of adherents, mostly in Valladolid and Seville, and even these were to all appearances totally wiped out by a series of *autos de fe* which the Inquisition held from 1559 onwards. Philip was present at the first of these, and is said to have told a victim: 'If my son were to oppose the Catholic Church, I myself would carry the faggots to burn him.' In these same years measures were taken to impose a rigid censorship on books and to prohibit Spaniards from studying abroad. These steps laid the basis for a system of intellectual control to which there were parallels in other countries but which in Spain was operated with a unique efficiency, through the Spanish Inquisition. Many Spaniards were naturally unhappy about limitations on their intellectual freedom, and there is indisputable evidence that some suffered. But the adverse influence of the Inquisition must be set against the major achievements attained by Spanish culture in the age of imperial greatness.

Spain after 1559 was living in the post-Erasmian era. The last prominent survivors of the Erasmian tradition, like Juan de Valdes – who was forced to flee to Italy – were too liberal to be tolerated. But the peninsular Counter-Reformation was not exclusively reactionary. It could point back to the reforms of Cardinal Cisneros as having laid the basis for a healthier Church, and in the mystical school of the late sixteenth century it produced a movement without equal in Europe. The poetic and contemplative genius of Luis de León, the mystical verse of St John of the Cross, were excelled only by St Teresa of Avila, whose contribution as reformer, mystic and woman of letters (she was also subsequently adopted as patron saint of Spain) gives her a universal greatness.

By the seventeenth century, only faint flickerings of Erasmianism remained, notably in the writings of Cervantes. Miguel de Cervantes

Defaced portrait of Erasmus from a copy of Sebastian Münster's *Cosmographia* (1550) brought into Spain.

Luis de León, scholar and poet of Jewish origin: he and other scholars were persecuted by the Inquisition for their humanist views and their use of Hebrew sources for Biblical studies.

(1547–1616), the first part of whose *Don Quixote* was published in 1605, dominated the literary achievement of the age. *Quixote* was a profoundly Spanish novel, but it also surveyed Spain's part in European history and the relevance of the Spanish situation to the universal human condition. Its author's popularity extended beyond the peninsula: in the Netherlands, for example, nineteen editions of works by him were published between 1607 and 1670. Cervantes was a critic of his times: *Quixote* reflects the many weaknesses and shams in Spanish society of the golden age. But writers were still conscious of the world role of their country. One wrote in 1584 that under Philip 'the time will come when the world admits one shepherd only and one monarchy'. Others took pride in the achievement of a host of distinguished writers and dramatists – Lope de Vega, Luis de Góngora, Tirso de Molina – who were to make this the great age of Castilian literature. There was another side to these writings, however. Awareness of the seamy aspects of the human condition created in Castile a new genre, that of 'picaresque' novels, which quickly became popular in other countries. A combination of satire and social

SCENOGRAPHIA
TOTIVS FABRICÆ
S·LAVRENTII
IN ESCORIALI·

Sixteenth-century engraving of the Escorial, the palace-monastery which Philip II used as a retreat from duties of state in Madrid.

Velázquez' portrait of Queen Mariana of Austria, wife of Philip IV.

realism, qualities that are found equally in *Quixote*, distinguishes these writings, of which the two most successful were the anonymous *Lazarillo de Tormes* (1554) and *Guzman de Alfarache* (1599), written by Mateo Alemán.

As in literature, Spaniards were at first heavily influenced by Italy in art, sculpture and architecture. Initially relying on Italian forms, they soon evolved a style of their own. In architecture the move to a purer Castilian style was first made by Juan de Herrera (d. 1597), creator of the Escorial, the immense and majestic palace-monastery that sits brooding in the mountains beyond Madrid. Herrera had been educated chiefly in Italy, but he began a native school which dominated Castilian architecture for half a century after his death. In sculpture the reigns of Philip II and his son coincide with a shift from an imaginative but severe Mannerism to a more popular and evocative style; both these approaches were Italian in origin, but they also reflected the change of mood in the Spanish religious and cultural temper. Under Philip III sculpture reflects a more fervid and popular religiosity, a sign perhaps of growing preoccupation with internal problems.

In painting El Greco (1541–1614) bestrides the period as the almost exact contemporary of Cervantes. He came to Spain only in the 1570s,

In the canvases of the Spanish mystical painters – El Greco, Zurbaran, Valdés Leal – we can see the profound spirituality of the Spanish mind in the sixteenth and seventeenth centuries, an inner vision that is also found in the writings of St Teresa and St John of the Cross.

Right, Valdés Leal (1622–90), *St Ignatius Loyola.*

Below, El Greco, *The Agony in the Garden*, 1585.

Opposite, Zurbaran, *St Serapion*, 1628

a thorough adept of the Venetian school of painting. Despite its Italian origins and close relation to contemporary Mannerism, Greco's art was intensely personal and Spanish, particularly in the overriding religious theme that dominates all his painting. He can be considered the last of the Spanish Mannerists before the advent of Baroque in the early seventeenth century. Baroque under Philip III and his son continued to emphasize the mysticism which is associated with El Greco. But it also included a secular realism that became basic to all the great Baroque painters. Ribera was one of the first to combine these two apparently conflicting themes, Velázquez was the greatest. Though best known for his court portraits, Velázquez (d. 1660) used his canvases to cover the whole range of social life, with a technical perfection and a respect for humanity that places him at the summit of the Spanish achievement during the Habsburg centuries. The irony is that this summit should have been attained in a time of political decline and psychological decay. The moral collapse of Spain, which begins at the time of the Thirty Years War, preceded by nearly half a century the evaporation of its immense cultural resources.

The ideals of this great age of culture shine through clearly in the plays and from the canvases: spiritual faith, personal honour, military heroism. They were ideals, above all, of the Castilian mind.

The reign of Philip II (1556–98) was the high-water mark of Spanish fortunes, but the problems of empire were also menacing. From his father Philip inherited rivalry with France, distrust of the Papacy, and hostility to Islam and Protestantism; in the course of his reign he also had to deal with a revolt in the Netherlands. These commitments meant that he was obliged to wage war against most other powers at some time during his reign. Spanish imperialism in Europe was consequently exercised in virtual isolation. It was a universal monarchy whose enemies were not limited to any one nation or religion. Catholic France, Protestant England and Muslim Turkey came to be its bitterest opponents. Spain was accordingly obliged to utilize all the resources of the peninsula and the overseas empire in an unflagging struggle to maintain its place in Europe. On the whole, the years up to the 1570s were successful. Despite occasional differences with the Pope, Philip proved himself a defender of Catholicism by his support of the Council of Trent (whose last session was in 1563). Spanish troops were moderately successful in the Netherlands; in 1570 they suppressed the *morisco* uprising in Granada; and they provided the main force for the navy that defeated the Turks at Lepanto (1571). Cervantes, who was wounded at this famous naval battle, described it as 'the greatest occasion that past or present ages have seen, or that future ones can hope to see'. In that same year a Spanish conquistador founded the city of Manila in the Philippines. Spain had now

The Water-Carriers of Seville, one of Velázquez' scenes of ordinary life that represent his greatest achievement.

Philip II, the 'Prudent King', a zealous Catholic devoted to the interests of his faith and country.

entrenched itself in the world's three greatest seas: the Mediterranean, the Atlantic, the Pacific. The decade ended with the conquest of Portugal in 1580, after a dispute over the throne. This had fallen vacant because of the death of the unfortunate King Sebastian in a crusading expedition into Morocco in 1578. With the unification of all Iberia under one Crown, Philip had reached the peak of his greatness.

After these years the descent from greatness was so inexorable that historians have become fascinated by it. Imperial difficulties were only one, but certainly the major, cause of the crisis. By committing itself too extensively, the Spanish war machine was doomed to repeated bankruptcies. First in 1557, and thereafter roughly every twenty years, the state repudiated its debts. The chief drain on men and money was the war against the Dutch rebels. 'The war in the Netherlands', a minister was to complain in 1623, 'has been the total ruin of this monarchy.' But though this was the greatest single liability, there were other no less serious commitments. The great 'enterprise of England', for example, whereby Philip had hoped to remove the English naval threat at one stroke by an invasion, collapsed with the failure of the

Fresco of the Battle of Lepanto, 1571, the most spectacular Christian success in the long struggle against the Turks for supremacy at sea.

Great Armada in 1588. Harassed by English ships in the Channel and ravaged by the weather, just over half the Armada managed to stagger back to Spain after a nightmare voyage round the north of the British Isles and the coast of Ireland. To defray the expenses of the disaster a new tax was imposed on Castile: this, the *millones*, was to become the most hated of all the taxes levied on an already heavily burdened population. As the foreign obligations multiplied, the internal deficit grew: such was the unhappy logic of imperialism when operated by an essentially poor country.

One of the chief problems was that virtually all the money for foreign policy came from Castile and America alone. What little was raised in Aragon or Italy was usually spent there. The financial and political autonomy of Aragon and the other non-Castilian realms stood in the way of attempts to raise money. Philip II, the 'Prudent King', as he was known, wisely did not attempt to alter the constitution of Aragon when it rebelled in 1591, encouraged by his former secretary, Antonio Perez. Not until the reign of Philip IV (1621–65) did a chief minister, the Count-Duke of Olivares, have the courage to propose that the

Philip IV, who inherited heavy burdens of financial debt and overseas military commitment, and, *opposite*, his influential, reforming prime minister, the Count-Duke of Olivares. Both portraits are by Velázquez, the court painter.

other realms of the monarchy should contribute together with Castile to general costs.

Imperialism was costly not only in terms of money but also of men. The Spanish soldier was stationed in garrisons and at battlefronts throughout Europe; he also garrisoned outposts in Morocco, America and the Philippines. The peninsula could not keep up the supply, even though the majority of troops serving under the Spanish flag were usually mercenaries. Manpower was being drained off to America and into the Church: the result was growing pressure for restrictions on emigration and on entry into the celibate religious orders. The countryside of Castile became more and more depopulated as a combination of harsh taxation and indebtedness drove the peasants to flee from the land and seek relief in the towns. Then, from about 1599, severe plague epidemics bit deeply into the population figures. As a consequence the early seventeenth century saw a disastrous fall in the population of Castile, aggravated still further by the expulsions of the *moriscos* in 1609.

There was a corresponding deterioration in Spain's military position. The Armada defeat was ominous, for in European waters Spain had let the initiative pass to the Protestant sea powers of the north. The Dutch provinces were thus ensured their independence. By the seventeenth century Dutch captains were raiding Spanish and Portuguese colonies in Asia and America, and Amsterdam replaced the Catholic cities as Europe's new commercial centre. English buccaneers ranged with increasing freedom in the Caribbean: to Americans Francis Drake became known as 'el Draco' ('the dragon'). Yet on land Spain was still the most powerful nation in Europe. As Philip IV put it in 1626: 'We have had all Europe against us, but we have not been defeated, nor have our allies lost, whilst our enemies have sued for peace.' Unfortunately, two years after this came the naval disaster of 1628 when, for the first time since the discovery of America, an entire treasure fleet was captured and its wealth carted off to Holland.

America played an equivocal role in Spanish history: it brought wealth, but also its attendant ills. Philip II was able to draw on the American mines to an extent undreamt of in his father's day. In the 1590s, when silver imports were at their peak, the bullion received by the Crown came to about one-fifth of the annual revenue of the treasury. This wealth was unfortunately poured out in an attempt to fill the bottomless well of military debts, and by the mid-seventeenth century the silver supply was dwindling to a trickle. Silver imports also had an unfavourable effect on the nation's economy. Easy profits from the American trade diverted investment from industry and the land. The inflow of bullion began to push up prices, and inflation affected both living standards and the costs of administration. The steepest rise

A piece of eight bearing the arms of Philip II.

was in the late sixteenth century, when prices rose by about 70 per cent. Then, from the early seventeenth century, the coinage was periodically devalued, and a century of monetary inflation ensued. The effect on the value of one unit of money, the *real*, was put thus by the seventeenth-century poet Francisco de Quevedo: 'The silver *real* says that he was worth four copper *reales* in the time of Don Ferdinand the Catholic; that the glorious emperor Charles V came along, and emergencies, or uprisings, or disorder (he is not sure which of these things it was) took one *real* away from him, and he was left with a value of three. Came Philip II, and another was taken away, and he was worth two. Came the lord king Don Philip III, and another *real* was taken away, and the silver *real* was worth one copper *real*.'

Unable to meet all foreign commitments, the ministers of Philip III, led by the Duke of Lerma, formulated a peace policy. Peace was signed with the English and a truce with the Dutch, in 1604 and 1609 respectively. It looked as though Spain were about to disengage from Europe. When events in Germany began to look threatening, the ministers refused to consider Spanish intervention. But the advent in 1621 of a new King, Philip IV, and a new prime minister, Olivares, changed matters. Olivares reversed the peace policy and supported Spanish involvement in what was to become the Thirty Years War.

It was (as many ministers argued) a costly mistake. Olivares's ministry was a distinguished one, notable for several serious attempts at reform; but he never solved the primary difficulty of finance.

His scheme for a 'Union of Arms' aimed to spread the burden of empire, both financially and militarily. The military provisions of the scheme suggested that each state of the Empire should maintain its own standing forces but could call on other states for assistance in emergencies. At the same time Olivares's scheme was intended to break down provincialism by allowing the different nationalities to participate more in the government of the Empire. But the attempt to realize the plan came to grief in Catalonia, where a major revolt broke out in 1640. It was not the only disaster of this period. In 1638 the French had captured the key Rhine fortress of Breisach, which controlled the supply route to the Netherlands. In 1639 a Dutch fleet had defeated the main Spanish naval force in the Channel. Then in 1640 no silver fleet arrived from America, a serious blow to the war treasury. Finally, in the wake of the Catalan uprising and the murder of the viceroy in Barcelona, came news from Portugal in 1640 of a revolt which was destined to free that nation permanently from Spanish control. 'This year', Olivares reported gloomily in September 1640, 'can undoubtedly be considered the most unfortunate that this monarchy has ever experienced.'

Miserable, ill-clad Spanish soldiers at the siege of Aire-sur-la-Lys, 1641, part of Spain's long and painful struggle to withhold independence from the Spanish Netherlands.

The riches supplied by the silver-mines of America were expended on military expeditions and extravagant secular and ecclesiastical decoration. Shown here are a reliquary, a casket and a monstrance, lavish and exquisitely wrought pieces made in the early seventeenth century.

Olivares was dismissed from his ministry early in 1643 and died two years later. Four months after his fall came news of the Spanish defeat by French forces at the Battle of Rocroi. The political and military stability of Spain appeared to be crumbling. The momentous years 1647–48 added to the gloom. In 1647 Sicily and Naples revolted against Spain, in 1648 a secessionist plot was uncovered in Aragon. In 1647 a terrifying epidemic of bubonic plague swept through the chief cities of Andalucia and Valencia, and in its wake came a wave of popular revolts against taxes. Abroad, in the peace conferences of 1648 that ended the Thirty Years War, Spain cut its losses and recognized at last the independence of the United Provinces. Catalonia was recovered in 1652, but Portugal had won its freedom finally, a fact recognized (again, only after much delay and further military expense) by treaty in 1668.

The period saw the last great flowering of 'golden age' art and culture. This was in no way a paradox, since art relied exclusively on patronage, and the years of political decline were *par excellence* the age of the wealthy, privileged patrons in the aristocracy, who now turned their attention from the arts of war to those of peace. The last of the great painters was Velázquez. Minor schools that existed after him, notably those of Valencia and Seville, were more local in vision and inspiration. Philip IV's reign was the great age of the playwrights, particularly Lope, Tirso and Alarcón; there are few of comparable stature in the following reign. Calderón's death (1681) marks the end of the great epoch of the Spanish theatre.

An unusual but in many ways typical figure on the literary scene was the poet Francisco de Quevedo (d. 1645), a prolific writer who at his death repudiated the greater part of his works. He was an accomplished satirist through whose eyes we can perceive the disillusion of many Spaniards with their rulers and with the society in which they lived. 'In your country', he wrote in 1604 to a correspondent in the Netherlands, 'we consume our soldiers and our gold; here we consume ourselves.' Quevedo represented a trend by which Spaniards, pessimistic about their country's destiny abroad, turned fiercely in on themselves and adopted ultranationalist and ultraconservative views. If Spain was decaying, men such as Quevedo argued, it was because of subversion by foreigners, Jews and heretics. Salvation for Spain lay in the traditional virtues of undiluted Christian blood and an unsullied Catholic religion. This kind of regressive thinking has often been blamed for the decline in Spanish artistic output in the course of the seventeenth century. But perhaps most notable of all is the *imbalance* rather than the regression in culture. Great emphasis came to be placed on faith and sentiment, less on reason. When Spain was glorying in its theologians and painters, in Loyola and Velázquez, England had produced Harvey, Italy Galileo, Holland Huyghens, France Pascal. Science and philosophy appeared to flourish everywhere save in Spain. This was not entirely true, since there were several wellknown experts in the live sciences and in technology, and the medical school of Valencia in particular could compare favourably with most other countries. But the names remained minor, as did Spain's contribution to modern European science. The Spanish universities by the time of Philip IV had become decadent and without academic distinction. The cultural achievements of the Habsburg centuries, great as they are, must therefore be set against the failure to evolve intellectually towards the new age.

Spanish writers of the time differed about the reasons for decay. Cellórigo, writing in 1600, argued that too easy wealth had ruined the country's industrial capacity. Navarrete, writing in 1626, stressed

the enormous foreign obligations of the Crown and the strange fact that Castile, unlike other imperial powers, seemed not to have bene-fited from the possession of an empire. Salazar y Castro, in 1687, deplored the loss of Castile's life-blood, its money: 'the court of Rome, the subsidies to Germany, the upkeep of Flanders, the wars in Milan and Catalonia, drain the blood out of this body through all its veins.' What really brought the crisis home to contemporaries was the glaring contrast between the might of Spain abroad and the poverty of Castile within. Abroad, the kings were obliged to pay their debts with silver, but at home they were forced to live off a debased copper coinage. The injustices of the social system served to intensify and perpetuate internal difficulties. The maldistribution of wealth was such, a writer of the early seventeenth century observed, that 'the people abandon the countryside for the towns, the poor become slaves

Extremes of wealth and poverty co-existed in Spain. Murillo's engraving depicts St Diego of Alcalá bringing food to the poor.

93

of the rich, and the rich intensify their pursuit of luxury and pleasure'. Towns and cities grew rapidly under the Habsburgs: in the course of the sixteenth century Seville and Toledo doubled their population, Madrid grew to ten times its original size. Nobles drifted to the capital from their estates, in search of advancement; impoverished peasants went in search of sustenance. Extremes of rich and poor remained for a long time, as foreign travellers reported, the most striking feature of society in the cities.

A large part of Spain's weakness derived from the incapacity of its leaders. The decreasing ability of the Habsburg kings, aggravated by inbreeding, was only partly compensated for by the emergence of chief ministers (*validos*) to control the government. Virtually all the *validos* of the seventeenth century, with the prominent exception of Olivares, were themselves dependent on the support of a noble faction. It is the unedifying history of these factions that plays an important part in the evolution of the Spanish state. Under Charles II (1665–1700), a permanent invalid with no perceptible will of his own, a prey to superstitious fancies, the rule of faction reached its apogee. The Madrid government became openly discredited among the élite of the peripheral provinces. This was the main reason why the King's rebellious half-brother, Don Juan José of Austria, was able during the earlier years of the reign to attract such great support for himself in the Crown of Aragon. At the same time, in Barcelona an active group of traders and nobles resolved to take their own destinies into their hands. The rebirth and revolt of the periphery was one of the most ominous signs of the passage of Spain into the modern period of history.

Charles II, monarch of an inward-looking Spain in decline, attends Mass: detail of a painting by Claudio Coello.

4

Enlightenment and Revolution

The eighteenth century, during which western Europe experienced the Enlightenment, was in Spain a century of extremely slow rebirth. The accession of a new dynasty made no immediate impact on the nation. Charles II died childless and willed the throne to Philip, Duke of Anjou, grandson of Louis XIV of France. The testament was immediately disputed by powers – mainly England, Holland and the Empire – hostile to a further extension of French might, and Europe was plunged into the War of the Spanish Succession (1702–13).

Castilians were on the whole overjoyed by the succession of the young seventeen-year-old King, which promised them a part in the achievements of Europe's greatest ruler. The provinces of the Crown of Aragon were more apathetic. This made it easier for the invading armies (principally English and German) to overrun half the peninsula. But the Franco-Spanish forces eventually won the day. On the specious pretext that the population of the Crown of Aragon had rebelled, Philip V abolished the constitutions or *fueros* of Aragon and established in their place the laws of Castile. With this measure (1707), claimed one contemporary Aragonese noble, 'arrived the time so desired by the Count-Duke of Olivares, for the kings of Spain to be independent of all laws save that of their own conscience'. For the first time in history, Castile and Aragon became one political unit, sharing the same administration, laws and taxes. The creation of one Spain was carried through, however, more in form than in spirit. Essentially an act of military violence, union was always resented by the eastern realms. The Catalans in particular resented the loss of their ancient constitution. Their defeat, with the fall of Barcelona in 1714, symbolized the defeat of regional separatism by centralist Castilian power.

Despite the radical turn of events during the War of Succession, the reign of Philip V was essentially one of quiet continuity. In Catalonia and Valencia, where Catalan was the main language, all public business was henceforward transacted in Castilian. Discontent was surprisingly muted, and all Spaniards grew to accept the Bourbons as their own. 'What was the whole of Spain before the august House of Bourbon came to the throne?' asked the eighteenth-century Catalan

Goya's *Superstition* from the sketchbook for *Caprices*, published in 1797.

97

Ceiling-tiles of the mid-eighteenth century showing traders at a Valencian port.

historian Capmany. 'A corpse, without spirit or strength to feel its own debility.' Peaceful internally, the reign was quite the reverse externally. An aggressive foreign policy meant that the forty-five years of Philip's reign (this includes the interlude of a year when he abdicated in favour of his son Luis) witnessed only ten years of peace. This warlike activity was a result of the Treaty of Utrecht (1713) which ended the War of Succession. By it, Spain gave up Italy and the Netherlands, and the English were ceded Gibraltar and Minorca. Deprived at one blow of control of the western Mediterranean, Spain devoted its energies to making good the loss and to rejuvenating its own internal administration. England, the rising power in the Mediterranean, now became for a century Spain's chief enemy. The rapid growth of the Spanish navy under Philip's greatest minister, José Patiño, was testimony to the nation's new energies under Bourbon rule.

The steady rise in population was a sign of better times. Imprecise figures suggest a growth from over six to eleven millions between 1700 and 1800. The increased labour force was recruited for the new factories set up during the war (textiles, munitions), for the army and for the expanding mercantile marine. Agricultural production increased considerably in the course of the century. An era of commercial capitalism dawned, as moneyed men explored new ways of putting their capital at the service of the state. Catalans and Basques attempted to set up trading companies, directed in part to the American trade.

An important part in this rebirth was played by the periphery. The Basque provinces on the northern coast were quietly surging ahead during the years of Castile's decline, and their loyalty during the War of Succession ensured them a continuity of privileges that the less fortunate Catalans lost. The Cantabrian coastline was the centre of Spain's fishing and shipbuilding industries; iron and steel production was important; the Basque ports controlled Castile's

98

export trade (especially in wool) to the north. With their freedom from the burdensome Castilian tax system, the Basques were in a position to seize industrial leadership. Despite the material damage suffered by Catalonia during the war, the Catalans too were in a position to expand. The symbol of Catalan resurgence was the booming seaport of Mataró, whose commerce was tied to the newly developing domestic industries of the interior. In Valencia a culturally progressive élite, including many distinguished scholars of medicine, was growing.

The early eighteenth century, a period long neglected by historians, was not merely a prelude to the Enlightenment. It exists in its own right as an epoch when significant steps were taken to end the cultural isolation in which the Habsburgs had kept Spain. The great official academies founded by Philip V (Spanish Royal Academy in 1713,

Four eighteenth-century traders – tailor, weaver, blacksmith, carpenter – as depicted on eighteenth-century ceramic tiles.

The royal palace at Aranjuez as it appears on a late eighteenth-century print.

Charles III is acclaimed in Madrid on his accession to the Spanish throne in 1759.

Royal Academy of History in 1738) were based on French models. The National Library of today (housed in a nineteenth-century building) was founded in 1711 as the Royal Library, incorporating books brought by the King from France and others confiscated from the libraries of rebellious nobles. The great new palaces built by Philip, such as La Granja (his 'Little Versailles'), or the Royal Palace in Madrid, were executed by Italian architects. Aranjuez, the other great palace of this period, had been started by Herrera in the sixteenth century, and was completed in the course of the eighteenth by French and native engineers. Italian styles proliferated under the early Bourbons, thanks to the connection established by Philip's marriage to the Italian Princess Elizabeth Farnese. Italian architects, sculptors, printers and musicians came to the court at Madrid. Scarlatti and Boccherini were among the eminent composers who visited Spain. Under their new dynasty, Spaniards – while not ceasing to develop their own skills – began to appreciate the achievements of other nations. This bred new standards of culture and erudition. One of the most outstanding products of the new outlook was the late eighteenth-century Valencian scholar Gregorio Mayans y Siscar. In the north of Spain, in Asturias, the writings of a Benedictine monk, Feijóo (d. 1764), were to be taken by the subsequent generation as a harbinger of Enlightenment philosophy. 'While abroad there is progress in physics, anatomy, botany, geography and natural history', Feijóo complained, in Spain there was a 'preoccupation against all novelty'. Through his works, Feijóo prepared the élite to accept foreign novelties, particularly the thinking of English and French writers.

The loss of the European empire made it possible for the government to turn its mind to internal reconstruction. A new bureaucracy was introduced into united Spain in the form of intendants; military academies were established, uniforms adopted; the navy was expanded into one of the most powerful in Europe; reforms in taxation were projected. Many of these ventures were the work of the remarkable chief minister of Ferdinand VI (1746–59), the Marquis of Ensenada.

Charles III (1759–88), Ferdinand's half-brother, had already been King of Naples for twenty-four years when he succeeded his brother on the Spanish throne. His mature age and long experience were to help make his reign in many ways the most brilliant in all Spanish history. Charles kept control of the Spanish state within his firm and capable hands; his ministers were servants, who could be dispensed with when necessary. He was the one king in eighteenth-century Spain who can be called an 'enlightened despot'. He was admittedly despotic in that his policies and reforms were often adopted without reference to public opinion ('My subjects', he said on one occasion, 'are like children: they cry when they are washed'); but he never went to extremes, and compromised readily. Strongly anti-English in his foreign policy, he continued the previous attempts to expel the English from Gibraltar and to restrict their presence in the Mediterranean.

The social advances under Charles III were achieved by a liberal, free-thinking élite. Well-educated nobles and ministers like Jovellanos and the Count of Campomanes were the spearhead of both political and economic reform. Other nobles maintained private cultural and scientific links with England, France, Sweden and other countries. Among them were the Count of Aranda, friend of Voltaire and Spanish ambassador to France; the Duke of Alba, friend of Rousseau and likewise ambassador to France; and the Count of Peñaflorida, who studied in France and later in 1765 joined a group of other Basque nobles to found the Basque Society of Friends of the Country (Amigos del País). Foreign books, such as the works of Locke, Rousseau, Newton and many others, were eagerly imbibed by Spaniards. It was impossible to check the growth of new ideas. On the notable occasion in 1778 when the Inquisition succeeded in imprisoning a leading government official, Pablo de Olavide, the confession of a friend of his implicated so many of the Crown's ministers that the Holy Office was obliged to let the matter drop. The Enlightenment in Spain drew heavily on French and foreign influences: a writer of the stature of Cadalso openly modelled his *Moroccan Letters* on Montesquieu's *Persian Letters*. But the Spaniards adapted foreign influences to their own tastes. All the

Charles III, Spain's enlightened despot. The portrait, by Goya, shows the King in hunting costume.

103

In 1766, the Jesuits, charged with arousing popular dissatisfaction, were expelled from Spain. *Above*, a popular print attacking the order as 'authors of pernicious leagues and plots'. *Opposite*, a group of Jesuits about to leave Spain.

great progressives remained firm Catholics, and officials of the Inquisition could be found among members of the economic societies of Amigos del País. As long as traditionalist forces coexisted, albeit uneasily, with the new trends, the government remained unworried. This explains why Charles III, when asked why he did not abolish the Inquisition, replied, 'the Spaniards want it, and it does not bother me'.

There were several clashes between the old and new. Church-state relations were made difficult by the active alliance of Jesuits and Inquisition against French influences and certain aspects of state policy. In these circumstances it was not surprising that when the government sought out those responsible for the popular riots in Madrid in 1766 against the widely hated Italian minister Squillace, it was the Jesuits who were chosen as the scapegoat. The extent of their alienation from the great forces in Church and state is shown by the fact that forty-six out of the sixty bishops voted for the decree, issued in 1767, to suppress the Society of Jesus and expel its members from Spain. The expulsion, and the evacuation of the great Jesuit colleges, enabled the government to proceed with another controversial measure, the reform of the universities. Olavide (who later fell foul of the Inquisition) in 1769 presented a plan for educational reform, which was adopted as the basis of the decree of 1770 reforming the syllabuses of all Spanish universities.

The economic progress of the late eighteenth century was notable.
A new attitude to economic growth was stimulated by the diffusion
of the economic societies of Amigos del País. Between 1765 and 1789
fifty-six societies were founded throughout Spain. Sponsored by
provincial nobility, their task was to promote technical knowledge
and encourage investment. The favourable economic climate of the
period had a beneficial effect on production, but little would have
been achieved without the crucial help given by state legislation.
Ministers pioneered the way with incisive studies of what was required, works such as Campomanes's two *Discourses on Industry*
(1774–75), and the famous analysis of Spanish agriculture (*Informe
de ley agraria*, 1795) written by Jovellanos. Government policy
directed the building of canals and roads, the equitable distribution of
land, the free internal trade of agricultural produce, the opening
of rural banking facilities, a ban on the acquisition of land by the
Church. In 1779 Campomanes was appointed head of the Mesta,
the sheep-owners' guild which had played a prominent part in
restricting agricultural growth, and he exploited his post by under-
mining the guild's privileges. Belief in freer trade led to a relaxa-
tion of the traditional monopoly system by which only Cadiz
and Seville had been allowed to trade to America. In 1765 and
1778 the American trade was progressively opened to all Spain's
major ports.

These steps gave a positive stimulus in particular to the periphery. In Valencia the silk industry expanded rapidly, from eight hundred looms in 1718 to five thousand in 1787, making it a major European producer. The iron and shipbuilding industries of the Basque provinces experienced boom conditions. But it was Catalonia that benefited principally: it forged ahead to the industrial leadership it was to attain in the following century. By the end of the eighteenth century it had a cotton industry second in size only to that of England. Much of this progress was related to the opening of the American trade, on which Catalonia was heavily dependent for raw cotton. In 1785 the directors of the state bank were able to express satisfaction in 'the progress of our industry, the multiplicity of modern factories in Catalonia, the extension of those in Valencia, the growth of agriculture, and the increase in demand for its products'. The centre of the peninsula, which had exercised leadership throughout the Habsburg centuries, now lost its primacy as the expansion in population and production shifted (as in ancient Hispania) to the periphery.

Agriculture, in which the overwhelming majority of the working population was engaged, remained stunted. The area of greatest agrarian distress, Andalucia, was the subject of reform projects that

Goya's allegories of Industry and Commerce, commissioned for Godoy's palace, and (*below*) two of his drawings from the Prado Sketchbook, *To the Market* and *Peasant Woman*.

failed largely because no steps were taken to alter the system of land-ownership. A rise in rents and prices in the late eighteenth century increased the misery of the landless rural labourers in the arid south. Jovellanos, surveying a typical depressed tract in Andalucia, asked rhetorically 'why so much poverty?'; then answered himself: 'because of the *baldíos* [common lands], because the lands are unfenced, because the village belongs to the duke of Alba, because of noble and ecclesiastical holdings'. Side by side with intellectual progress there was an alarmingly rapid deterioration in the condition of the lower classes both in the countryside and in the towns. This poverty contrasted starkly with the wealth of the upper orders in Church and state. The Church had too many clergy and too much money. As the owner of vast estates (in Galicia it owned half the territory) it was often directly responsible for the poverty of labourers. There was good ground for the anti-clericalism that has become a common feature of Spain's modern history.

Despite progress in many fields, the social problem remained unsolved. Castile was slow to provide leadership. The great reforming ministers were non-Castilians: Ensenada came from Logroño, Campomanes and Jovellanos from Asturias, the Count of Floridablanca from Murcia. Castilian literature blossomed with writers like Leandro Moratín (d. 1828), a distinguished playwright well acquainted with foreign culture. But the cultural rebirth of non-Castilian Spain was perhaps even more notable: in medicine the outstanding names included the Catalans Gimbernat and Casal, in natural history the Valencian Cavanilles, in economics the Catalan Capmany. The foreign artists Mengs and Tiepolo were the most influential at court, and when the native genius of Spain broke through it was in the stupendous canvases of the Aragonese painter Francisco Goya (1746–1828). Goya's vast output and his wide range of themes mercilessly caricatured every aspect of Spanish character; at the same time he managed to convey the underlying strength and vision of Spain in all its moods, from the bright sunshine of the bull-fight to the savage heroism of the War of Independence.

Under the eighteenth-century Bourbons many of the customs for which Spain is well known to tourists came into regular use. The construction of fine leafy avenues in Madrid (the spacious Prado promenade) and in Barcelona (the Rambla) brought out the men in their French-style costumes and the ladies in their native but no less stylish gowns. On these walks, or *paseos*, the ladies would flaunt their charms, flutter their fans, and flirt with the gallants. The avenues and the coaches were all French in style. But, as if in reaction to these foreign imports, native styles of popular origin sprang up and were readily adopted by high-born ladies. The emphasis on 'authenticity',

View of the Rambla in Barcelona.

or *casticismo*, can be seen most clearly in the feminine fashions in contemporary paintings. It provided a sense of public identity which Castilians in particular were willing to adopt. The young lower-class dandies of Madrid, known as *majos*, sported a distinctive dress and swagger, while their ladies, *majas*, outdid them in flamboyance. Traditions that were essentially native to Andalucia spread rapidly and became identified with Spanishness: bullfighting, for example, became a national pastime, flamenco song and dance became a popular art form.

Charles III had given Spain a new spirit internally and a new strength abroad. His vigorous anti-English maritime policy was most successful in North America, where he actively supported the colonists in their struggle for independence. His son and successor, Charles IV (1788–1808), had little opportunity to display his rather limited talents, for the year after his accession coincided with the outbreak of the French Revolution. All the efforts of his prime minister, Floridablanca (a former progressive who had also been a chief minister of Charles III), were devoted to sealing off the peninsula

Two scenes of life in eighteenth-century Spain. *Above*,
Goya's lithograph of bullfighting, *The Divided Arena*,
and, *opposite*, the interior of an
inn in Valencia.

against Jacobin influence. Floridablanca's successor, the Count of
Aranda (who had been chiefly responsible for the expulsion of the
Jesuits in the previous reign), held on to power very briefly. At the
Queen's instance, his place was soon taken by her handsome favour-
ite, a young man of doubtful ability named Manuel Godoy.

The Spanish government did what it could to shield Spaniards
from the world-shaking impact of the French Revolution, but though
a heavy curtain of censorship was drawn it was never as effective as
in the sixteenth century. The presence of a large French colony in the
trading centres of Spain, and the volume of commerce with France,
meant that information was bound to filter through. To combat this,
Frenchmen were compelled to become Spanish citizens or leave the
country. Their departure was countered by the arrival in Spain of

thousands of French refugees (by 1793 over six thousand French clergy alone had reached Spain). Floridablanca went to extreme lengths to stop any news of events in France reaching Spain. In 1791 he annihilated the intellectual movement by a decree which suspended all private periodicals. Aranda's rather milder ministry could not afford to relax the restrictions because of the active republican propaganda coming from France. In the peninsula political excitement had been stirred up to a high pitch. One contemporary reported that in Madrid, 'in the inns and over the tables you hear of nothing but battles, revolution, convention, national representation, liberty and equality'. However, the growth of pro-French sentiment was rapidly dampened by the news first of the execution of Louis XVI (1793) and then of the beginning of the Jacobin Terror.

Portraits by Goya of Charles IV and his family and, *opposite*, of Manuel Godoy, who as one of Charles IV's chief ministers – and the Queen's favourite – played a decisive role in Spanish politics.

After the King's execution, the Revolutionary Convention in Paris declared war against Spain. It was one of the most popular wars in Spanish history: all classes and the whole nation were united in their detestation of the republicans. Regional patriotism, particularly that of the Basques and Catalans, was aroused for Spain against the foreigner. Though French forces managed to penetrate Spain, their progress was halted by the Treaty of Basel (1795), by which Spain gave up Santo Domingo to France. The next year Godoy was obliged to sign a treaty of alliance with France against England. This disastrous agreement, which drew down on Spain England's far superior naval power, began the break-up and loss of Spain's overseas territories. Trinidad was annexed by Britain at this period. In 1797 the impossibility of protecting America against British aggression forced Spain to cut the colonies free and allow them to trade with neutral powers. South America was now for all practical purposes lost to Spain, which never regained control.

Internally the government faced a critical situation. Military burdens crippled the treasury, and while government credit crumbled the cost of living soared. Between 1780 and 1800 a labourer's wages rose by only 12·5 per cent while the price level rose by 50 per cent.

When Napoleon became First Consul of France in 1799, he increased his demands on Spain. A treaty in 1800 forced the government to cede Louisiana (in effect, most of Spain's territory in North America) to France. Bullied by France and harassed by the English, Spain was also suffering internally from economic difficulties and epidemics. In 1804 the government declared war on Britain. The next year brought the great Franco-Spanish naval disaster at Trafalgar.

It was clear that subservience to France was ruining Spain. In Madrid Charles IV found that the French alliance had in reality become a French occupation. The annexation of Portugal by French troops in 1807 was followed by the imposition of French garrisons on Spanish cities in 1808, when General Murat took over control of Spain. Differences over policy at court led to disagreements between Charles and his son Ferdinand, who mounted the throne as Ferdinand VII in March 1808 after Godoy had been displaced and Charles forced to abdicate. The French command refused to recognize the change of monarch, and the royal family was induced to go to Bayonne, just inside the French frontier, to lay their differences before Napoleon. Once at Bayonne, Charles and Ferdinand were in Napoleon's power. The latter persuaded Ferdinand to renounce the

CARO HERMANO PRISIONEROS CON EL. FERNANDO VII.º R. DE L. E. DESCONSOLADO EN SU PRISION DE FRANCIA OYE LOS CONSEJOS DESU TIO Y LAS DOLOROSAS QUEJAS DESU

Crown but immediately made Charles surrender it to France. Napoleon then chose his brother Joseph as the new King of Spain.

The economic distress of these years made popular unrest inevitable. When in addition the people of Madrid found that Murat had seized control from the royal family, they registered their protest on 2 May 1808 – the *Dos de Mayo*, immortalized in Goya's canvases – by rising against the French army of occupation and so setting ablaze the War of Independence. Most historians adopt the year 1808 as the beginning of Spain's modern history, and with good reason. The popular uprising at Aranjuez on 17 March, when Godoy's palace was sacked (the favourite was found hiding in a rolled-up carpet) and Charles forced to abdicate after dismissing Godoy, signalled the first violent irruption of the masses on to the field of Spanish politics. The revolt of 2 May, tragic in its consequences, confirmed the leadership of the common people in the forthcoming struggle.

Almost without a signal from their leaders, the Spanish people rose against the intruders. 'My position is unique in history,' Joseph wrote to Napoleon, 'I have not a single supporter here.' Asturias was

Within the illustration: Constitución Españo[la] / El Tio Pepe Botella's / chara d Tetuan. / 1°. All que tra baſes por ſ / vez ſe le dara una ſuria / y ſi rei.n.cle.r.... / Proyecto para hacer de / España una nueva Tauja / ó la isla de Cucaña

Opposite, popular print depict-ing Ferdinand VII imprisoned by the French, and, *left*, *A Patriot from La Mancha* ex-presses his contempt for French efforts to reform the political structure of Spain.

the first province to rise, to be followed by the whole nation. A dele-gation to London brought the British in on the side of Spain. It was both a heroic and a brutal war. Goya's etchings *The Disasters of War* capture vividly the extreme cruelty and savagery which were never to be absent from subsequent conflicts in the nineteenth and twentieth centuries. Because of the bravery of Spaniards in the War of Indepen-dence, there has been a tendency among older historians to idealize their position. The reality was a little more complex. Most placed their hopes in the absent Ferdinand, their 'Desired One' (*el Deseado*). But beyond that there was a division into roughly two attitudes. For the mass of the people and for the upper levels of society, the war was a conservative one in defence of tradition, religion and local rights. France for them represented impious republicanism and wicked atheism. Despite being firmly wedded to such traditional values, the common people were frequently also capable of spontaneous acts of ferocity against the upper classes. The other principal attitude, held by a small minority, resented French aggression but was sympathetic to many French ideas. People in this group looked forward to the day

One of Goya's etchings for his *Disasters of War* series.

Two popular prints from a series recounting the siege of Saragossa by French forces in August 1808. *Above*, the Countess of Bureta, heroine of the siege and, *right*, the governor of the citadel with his men.

after liberation when the reforms and enlightenment of the eighteenth century could be extended. Here essentially was the split into 'two Spains' – traditionalist on one side, reformist on the other – that set the pattern for all subsequent Spanish history.

Spain was split even further by the breakdown in public authority. Because Spaniards refused to recognize the French government in Madrid, control reverted to the local level. Regionalism received a massive stimulus. Each area set up a provincial junta with sovereign powers, and the country broke into federal units, the only centre being a weak supreme Central Junta at Aranjuez. The French found themselves fighting not one concerted war but a series of fragmentary actions against Catalans, Valencians, Asturians and so on. Their operations were bogged down by having to fight off sporadic guerrilla attacks, and to conduct sieges of individual towns and cities. The difficult Spanish campaign (Napoleon was later to attribute the beginning of all his ills to intervention in the peninsula) forced the Emperor himself to march into the country. Spaniards were less effective in pitched battles, at which they were poor, than in guerrilla warfare. For the former they relied on the all-important aid of British troops under the Duke of Wellington. Together both British and Spaniards drove out most of the French by the end of 1813.

But the war had created a serious split in Spanish ranks. A number of enlightened liberals had supported French rule as the only way to implement reform. Many of them were former ministers of Charles III. When the French were expelled the liberals (to a total of twelve thousand families) were also obliged to leave. In 1810 there opened in Cadiz a *cortes* representing all the parts of Spain not occupied by French troops. The great work of this historic assembly was the famous Constitution of 1812, the first break made with tradition by the middle classes of Spain, and the future rallying-point of all liberal aspirations. The split between parties appeared in the open, chiefly over the question of abolishing the Inquisition. The Holy Office was in effect abolished in 1813, after two years of discussion, by ninety votes to sixty. It was resurrected under later régimes, but suppressed once and for all in 1834. Although the *cortes* was largely ineffectual, since it commanded neither troops nor territory, its work was important. A decree of 1811 which abolished feudal landholdings in Spain was epoch-making. The *cortes* was the first constitutional body in Spanish history to allow representatives from the American states to sit in it. The 1812 Constitution, moreover, was not merely the conservative document it professed to be: it was based on the French Constitution of 1791 and included many innovations such as the restriction of noble privileges and the establishment of a strictly constitutional monarchy.

The end of the War of Independence in 1814 brought the return of the 'Desired One', but raised problems as well. The French occupation had brought about major changes in the state, and had opened up an irreconcilable gulf between the liberals and the conservatives. Ferdinand VII chose to follow the old absolutist path, and began his new reign by abolishing the Constitution and imprisoning members of the liberal opposition. The Crown commanded great prestige thanks to its attitude in the war, and Ferdinand managed with some success for a few years, during which all the apparatus of the old régime was brought back. Below this repressive surface the differing political aspirations of Spaniards continued to seethe. The liberals strengthened their links with the army; secret societies such as the Freemasons became the resort of underground parties. This was a situation that was bound to produce extremes both of repression and of revolutionary violence, so setting the tone for nineteenth-century politics.

In 1820 a Colonel Riego raised the flag of military rebellion in Andalucia. It was the first full-scale *pronunciamiento* (the term is discussed in the next chapter) of modern times. Riego's stand was for the Constitution. When risings for the same cause occurred elsewhere, Ferdinand gave in and accepted the men of 1812. But the liberal success led immediately to a split in their ranks between the moderates and the radicals. This weakened their cause within Spain. Abroad the proclamation of the 1812 Constitution by Italian liberals aroused the anxiety of those European powers opposed to constitutional government. When the administration at Madrid fell into the hands of the radical liberals, there was widespread hostility to their harsh policies. This supplied the pretext for the French to send armed help to the royalists. The 'Hundred Thousand Sons of St Louis' (a phrase of Louis XVIII) entered the country in 1823 and helped Ferdinand to resume full absolute power and to abolish all liberal legislation. Counter-revolutionary terror claimed its toll of lives as the liberals went into exile. Once again the pattern of modern Spanish politics was being set. The victorious conservatives, however, found that matters were still not wholly to their liking. Ferdinand relied to some extent on moderate counsels, so that the extreme rightists began to place their hopes rather on his younger brother Carlos. The birth of a daughter and heir to Ferdinand in 1830 dashed royalist hopes that Carlos might succeed to the throne, but since Philip V had in 1713 introduced a law excluding females from the succession it was held by many that Carlos was still the legitimate heir. This created a succession dispute, and also a Carlist party (modern Carlists still claim that their branch of the Bourbon family should succeed to the Spanish throne).

Portrait of Ferdinand VII, *el Deseado*, by Goya.

The burial of the Serviles: Spanish print of about 1820 calling on the liberals to suppress the Serviles, royalist supporters of the absolutist king, Ferdinand VII.

Illustration from a ballad in commemoration of the soldiers who died suppressing the 1821 rising in Catalonia.

ENTIERRO DE   LOS SERVILES.

Ferdinand's reign left major problems for Spain. Both economically and politically the country was in a precarious state. Political labels meant little: 'moderates' were no less extreme in their resort to brutal repression than their enemies. Absorbed in domestic affairs, the King was powerless to stop the loss of the American colonies.

The occupation of Spain by French armies after 1808 had given the Americans a pretext for declaring their independence from the Franco-phile government in Madrid. But loyalty to Ferdinand soon changed into separatism. First Venezuela in 1811, then other states later, declared their independence. Upon the restoration of Ferdinand the American rebels were faced with the return of Spanish control. At this point the Venezuelan General Simón Bolívar, named 'the Liberator' by his country in 1814, undertook leadership of the struggle for independence. Helped by Britain and the United States, and by commanders such as San Martín, the Americans began a systematic overthrow of Spanish power. At Ayacucho in 1824, Bolívar's lieutenant Sucre crushed the last Spanish resistance. Save for Cuba and Puerto Rico, all southern Spanish America was free.

5

The Liberal Century

Spain was thrust reluctantly into the nineteenth century and has never quite emerged from it. The liberals claimed to be constitutionalists, but were no less eager than their opponents to force minority programmes through by force. The habit of violence became a permanent feature of Spanish politics. When the infant Isabella II succeeded to the throne in 1833 under the Regency of her mother, the dispute over the succession immediately burst into war. Most of the north of Spain rose in rebellion on behalf of their 'king', Don Carlos. It was the first great civil war in Spain since the fifteenth century. Carlism was a recurrent phenomenon that persisted through the nineteenth century. Its main support came from the strongly Catholic provinces of Navarre and Biscay and from the northern parts of Aragon and Catalonia, but it was never simply a regional or even a dynastic movement. Had it been so, it would have faded rapidly. In fact, Carlist sympathizers could be found all over the country. A mixture of various ideals and aims, the movement is best described simply as a reaction of traditionalist elements in Catholicism to the political tendencies of the new century. As such, it was truly a nation-wide movement, and had enough vigour to keep the civil war going until 1839, when the struggle ended in military compromise.

Though the civil war was ferocious, the ferocity of the Carlists themselves became proverbial. They revived the sinister secret society called 'The Exterminating Angel', a tool of clerical reaction first formed under Ferdinand VII. Priests led troops in committing extreme barbarities. Dwindling successes finally forced the Carlist General Maroto to come to terms with the royal General Espartero. Carlism ceased to be a major military threat after 1840, despite its continued political importance. Basque and Catalan adherents in particular channelled their energies into regionalism, always their chief interest.

Carlism's greatest enemy was 'liberalism', but the civil wars merely strengthened the hold of liberals on the government. Looking back, we can see that 'liberalism' was the sum total of a wide variety of policies. Clericals equated liberalism with Freemasonry, and with good reason. First introduced by the English in the eighteenth century, Masonry appealed to deist progressives; in the nineteenth century it drew on

The nineteenth century was Spain's century of revolutions. This lithograph shows the murder of General Bassa during the 1835 revolt in Barcelona.

Above, cartoon of 1828 satirizing the Carlist pretender, Don Carlos, as the assassin of Catalonia.

Right, contemporary print showing the sacking of the Santa Catalina convent in Barcelona, July 1825.

French influences. The Riego uprising was the first major one to be hatched in a Masonic cell. But though liberals continued to exploit the clandestine organization of Masonry for their own purposes, Masons never again directed the fortunes of liberalism to the same extent. The Carlists also saw liberalism as outright anti-clericalism, and could point to the events that occurred at the time of Mendizábal's Church policies (which are touched on below). Most liberals were certainly against Church privilege, but equally most were stoutly believing Catholics. The internal contradictions of the liberals opened up after 1820 when they split into 'moderates' and '*exaltados*' (democratic radicals), two streams that represented the men of property and the urban progressives respectively.

It was the men of property – industrialists in Barcelona and Bilbao, aristocrats and traders in Cadiz – who looked to liberalism for guarantees of an adequate civil liberty and an adaptable legal structure (abolition of old privileges, such as in 1811, but protection of newer property rights). They gave Spanish liberalism the peculiar significance of being, as Raymond Carr observes, an 'attempt to apply, by

An incident on the Rambla during the 1835 uprising in Barcelona.

means of military sedition, the politics of interest and the machinery of parlimentary government to an underdeveloped society'. The progres-sives, on the other hand, represented the liberalism of the streets, which rallied instinctively round the Constitution of 1812. Even they, with their democratic aspirations, were obliged to force liberty on to the unwilling majority. 'The Constitution of 1812', a liberal army officer declared, 'was made entirely for the people, but they hated it.' The solution chosen was to break any opposition by military means. When the 1812 Constitution was thought unsuitable, liberal leaders continued to pursue a belief in the necessity of constitutions by drawing up others in 1837, 1845 and 1868.

Political movements of the nineteenth century tended to function independently of political life in the capital, Madrid. The key to most of the issues in the 1830s, as later in the 1930s, lay in local and regional aspirations and struggles. The big parties, both left and right, relied for their credibility on the support of the urban bourgeoisie and the rural privileged throughout Spain. When they wished to carry out a *coup*, the Madrid politicians looked for the spark of revolution to an uprising, whether military or civil, in the provinces. Moreover, in a country rampant with regionalism, Madrid was seldom considered as the capital. The word *país* (country) applied not to the nation but to one's own little place of origin, a usage that is still commonplace. Government from a centre was therefore at best a patchy affair.

Carlist excesses made it easier for liberal anti-clericals to carry out their policies. Urban mobs demonstrated their dislike of clericalism by killing clergy and sacking convents in 1834–35. It was the first symptom of the chasm that was opening between the Spanish clergy and people. In 1836–37 the prime minister, Mendizábal, carried through a measure that the statesmen of the eighteenth century would dearly have loved to introduce: he nationalized all monastic property, began sales of Church land, and abolished entail. This *desamortización* or dissolution of Church wealth was a momentous event, comparable perhaps to the material impact of the Reformation on England. At one stroke all Church land was seized by the state, all religious orders were suppressed, many churches and monasteries vanished (in Madrid alone forty-four were levelled). It was the lowest point ever reached by the Spanish Church in all its history. Pushed through by the progressive liberals, the *desamortización* was disapproved of by the moderates. But the threat to property rights that they feared did not materialize. Carried out properly, the attack on the Church could have contributed to a solution of the profound agrarian problem. Instead, as the modern Catalan historian Jaime Vicens Vives has observed, 'it did nothing more than transfer property from the Church to the economically strongest classes (large landholders, aristocrats,

Caricature of Mendizábal sel-ling off Church property.

and bourgeoisie) – a development from which the state derived the least benefit and one which did grave harm to the agricultural workers'. The result can still be seen today in southern Spain. A system of *latifundia* (great estates), surpassing those created in the Middle Ages, was added to and extended. In the process, a large section of the propertied classes found themselves bound to the cause of Isabella II and liberalism.

On the surrender of the Carlists in 1839, Espartero (a progressive) was hailed as a hero and was named Duke of Victory (La Victoria). Disputes in the government brought about the Queen Regent's abdication and self-exile in 1840, whereupon Espartero was chosen as interim Regent. His Regency was singularly unsuccessful, and the moderates plotted vigorously to undermine the government. These events led in 1843 to uprisings throughout Spain, led by moderate generals such as Narváez and Prim. Espartero took ship for London. Political change had once again been carried through by the army.

Throughout the nineteenth century and down to today the army has been the supreme arbiter of Spanish politics. The liberals used the *pronunciamiento* as their principal means of revolution. Beginning as a plot among a small group of officers, the *pronunciamiento* aimed to enlist the sworn support of selected colleagues and sergeants. At the key moment the 'pronouncing' officers would address their assembled

Espartero, Duke of Victory, enters Barcelona in triumph on the final surrender of the Carlists in 1839.

troops and outline the reasons for their action: this was the *grito* or 'cry' of insurrection. In a *pronunciamiento* the army always kept the initiative: politicians were of secondary or no concern. The officers believed that they, and not the quarrelling politicians, were the ultimate repositories of the nation's will. The democratic origin of many of the officers (the army, like the Church, was one of the most important channels of social mobility) gave them a profound disdain for both aristocrats and plebeians. As men of action, they were particularly hostile to intellectuals, whom they consistently saw as anti-national. Though the generals often managed to gauge popular feeling accurately, they were more often too impatient of dissonant factors such as regionalism (from Espartero down to Franco they found Catalonia a constant thorn in their side) and the democratic process (demands for a free press and elections). Because it was shallow in its origins and support, a *pronunciamiento* never offered any solid solution to civil problems.

After Espartero's fall, Isabella at thirteen years was proclaimed of age by the moderates. Her reign proper now began. It was based on an extremely conservative new constitution, promulgated in 1845. Narváez acted as a military watchdog while several ministers

Banquet held by members of the progressive party, 1863.

Textile design showing Queen Isabella, accompanied by her consort and her son, the future King Alfonso XII, arriving at the Industrial Exhibition held in 1860 in Barcelona.

and governments succeeded each other. Despite continuing political instability, this was a period of real success for the liberal upper classes and for Spain. There was a striking and steady growth of population. The total increased from about eleven million in 1800 to sixteen in 1860, the highest rate of growth being in Catalonia. Introduction of the smallpox vaccine by way of Catalonia in 1800 may help to explain the favourable figures there. It was the astonishing increase in both agricultural and industrial output that provided the most favourable arguments for liberalism. Greater produce from the soil, particularly in the years after *desamortización*, made Spain generally self-sufficient in cereals. In Catalonia, where the wars and the loss of America had brought a decade of depression, manufacturers had by the 1830s expanded the cotton industry and a few years later were using steam-power. Barcelona became 'the Manchester of Spain'. The laws that had abolished entail and wrested land from the Church set new trends in motion: a more mobile property market, the possibility of urban improvements. Landed and industrial interests combined to support the régime which blessed their enterprises.

Narváez's tough military rule ('I have no enemies,' he claimed on his deathbed, 'I have shot them all') aroused discontent even within the ranks of the ruling moderates. The revolutionary events of the year 1848 in Europe, and the plots which occurred at the same time in Spain, aggravated by a resurgence of Carlism in Catalonia, made him resort to open dictatorship. He was followed in the premiership by

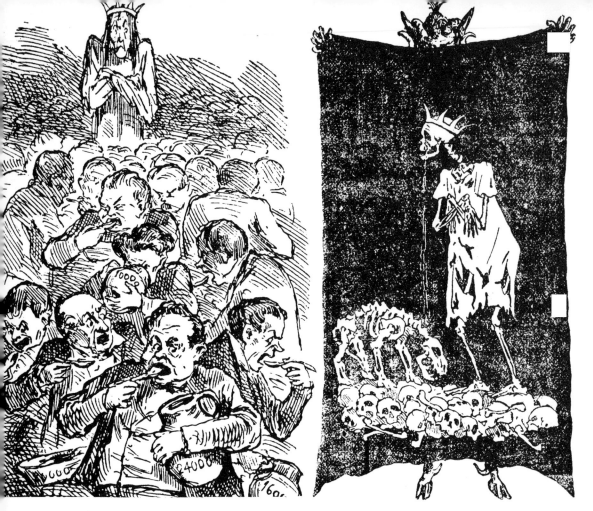

Spain Today and *Spain To-morrow*. Two cartoons of 1870 attacking profiteers and financiers.

more easy-going men, but opposition from all sides and from within the moderate party culminated in 1854 in another major *pronunciamiento*, led this time by General Leopoldo O'Donnell.

The successful *coup* brought about the recall of Espartero to head a new government. A coalition between him and O'Donnell, a moderate, was bound to be uneasy. Co-operation between the two liberal parties began hopefully with the summoning of a constituent assembly, but then more radical popular forces began to find their voice. In 1855 a general strike, the first in Spanish history, took place in Catalonia; in 1856 there was a workers' uprising in Barcelona. Isabella got rid first of Espartero, then of O'Donnell. Later O'Donnell came back in a moderate-dominated ministry.

The next twelve years saw the failure of the liberals to come together in any viable grouping. Government became openly conservative as radical aspirations were systematically repressed. The government won enormous popularity by overseas colonialist adventures in Morocco, Mexico and Indo-China. The capture in 1860 of Tetuán

Catalan woodcut of 1873 expressing popular support for a federal republic.

(Morocco) stirred dreams of imperial greatness. These exercises diverted attention from the serious political situation at home. Isabella refused to accept a progressive ministry and thereby committed the radicals to revolution as their only resource. Moderate government became more repressive and eventually under Narváez blossomed into full military dictatorship. In 1867 O'Donnell died, in spring 1868 Narváez. Isabella's two principal pillars had disappeared.

Meanwhile the opposition had been growing. Throughout the period of moderate government, General Prim in Catalonia had been looked on as one of the progressive hopes. In four years he attempted seven unsuccessful *pronunciamientos*. His persistence earned him leadership of the revolutionary conspiracy which in September 1868, after extensive and careful preparations, 'pronounced' against the government. A wave of revolutions swept over the country. Isabella, her position defenceless, left San Sebastian for France. The 1868 Revolution was more than just a successful *pronunciamiento*, and had deeper causes than Isabella's imprudent love-life. The year 1867 was one of

Caricatures of the various political factions in Spain.
Left to right, republicans, clericals, and the strange trinity of Carlist, anarchist and bourgeois.

'In time this child will know as much as I do.' Cartoon satirizing King Alfonso XII's efforts to master constitutional theory.

serious European depression; in the peninsula there was industrial recession and soaring price inflation. In Andalucia wheat was selling at six times the average price. Political resentment and agrarian misery united both towns and countryside against the régime. A provisional government was set up under Generals Serrano and Prim. The singular novelty of this military revolution was that it immediately accepted a new constitution with sweeping democratic concessions – votes for all, a free press, liberty of worship. Wider suffrage altered the character of politics: a new Republican party emerged, with a secure base in the provinces.

The problem of finding a new king was solved when Amadeo of Savoy, son of the King of Italy, accepted the throne. A reluctant monarch, his task was made no easier by civil wars (the Carlists in the Basque country and Navarre rose again), ministerial rivalry (the progressives split into a radical faction under Ruiz Zorrilla and a conservative one under Sagasta), popular agitation (socialist and anarchist agitators were at work in Andalucia and Catalonia), and the assassination of Prim, which occurred just as Amadeo was about to set foot on Spanish soil. He soon abdicated, and a republic was proclaimed in 1873.

The First Spanish Republic was headed by eminent and scholarly presidents such as the Catalan 'federalist' Pi y Margall and the republican Emilio Castelar. The government had an overriding commitment to decentralize the state into regional governments on a federal basis. But this aroused strong opposition in several quarters. After a few bare months of existence a *coup* in Madrid put an end to the Republic in 1874. The Carlists took advantage of the disorder to rise and attempt to impose their royal candidate on the country. Conservatives meanwhile were working to restore the Bourbons. At the end of December

Catecismo en imágenes.

tres personas distintas

1874, at Sagunto (in Valencia), General Martínez Campos uttered a *grito* against the Republic and proclaimed Isabella's son Alfonso XII, then sojourning in London, as King of Spain.

The Restoration (1875–1923) was the first great conservative attempt to erect a stable political system. The chief statesman of the early Restoration, Cánovas del Castillo, attempted to create a political consensus among all parties on the right. Influenced by British models, he accepted constitutional monarchy as the norm, and obliged the King to read Bagehot. Fortunately he secured the collaboration of the liberal leader Praxedes Sagasta. Co-operation between these groupings produced the most stable period of government that nineteenth-century Spain experienced. The constitution of 1876 formalized the joint rule of king and *cortes*. It also secured a system by which at the centre the two constitutional parties, liberals and conservatives, alternated in power peacefully (the *turno pacífico*), while in the provinces political

The Spanish-American crisis. Discussing the news from America in Madrid.

Opposite, conservative cartoon satirizing three short-lived presidents of the Federal Republic of 1873. From left to right: Pi y Margall (president April–June) depicted as a statue of Proudhon; Emilio Castelar (September–December) as a Freemason; and Nicolás Salmerón (July–September) as under the influence of Krause and Jacobinism.

Patriotic design recalling in defeat Spain's past military glories.

control lay in the hands of local party bosses (*caciques*). Cánovas's system was to some extent successful: the Carlists were pacified, traditionalist Catholics were won over, military *pronunciamientos* were conspicuous failures, liberal achievements such as universal suffrage and press freedom were absorbed painlessly. But the liberal-conservative oligarchy failed to make political life keep in step with economic and social realities. In particular, the evolution of working-class pretensions threatened to overcome the apparent stability of constitutional monarchy. The greatest disaster to Cánovas came from the Spanish-American War, when Spain in 1898 lost to the United States its last great colonial possessions – Cuba, Puerto Rico and the Philippines.

Defeat in 1898 was both a humiliation and a catastrophe. The extinction of the Spanish Empire, on which so many centuries of national pride had been nurtured, provoked an economic and psychological crisis. The industrial periphery was severely hit: Barcelona had had 60 per cent of its external trade with Cuba. The psychological reaction came in a wave of criticism directed against the political practices and intellectual values of the Restoration. A group of radical intellectuals, known commonly as 'the generation of '98', set out to analyse the reason for Spain's disaster, and to search for a solution to 'the Spanish problem'. Virtually all were Castilians, few were content to adopt the trimmings of modern European civilization as an adequate answer to Spain's difficulties.

Spain on the eve of the twentieth century was in a mood of doubt and questioning. This was possible only because of the serious advances that had taken place in the economy and culture of the nation. By the mid-nineteenth century the country appeared to be on the verge of an industrial revolution. In Catalonia the textile factories, in the Basque country the iron industry, were the spearheads of progress. Industrial Barcelona grew from 88,000 inhabitants in 1818 to 510,000 by 1897. The railway system expanded rapidly: in 1855 less than five hundred kilometres had been laid down, by 1900 the figure exceeded twelve thousand kilometres. Exports of agricultural produce increased. Much of this progress was attributable to foreign investment. English money began systematic exploitation of the Rio Tinto copper-mines, French money controlled most of the booming railway system, English investors encouraged Andalucian viticulture so that sherry could be produced. Foreign investment did not, of course, work entirely to the advantage of Spaniards: outsiders were quick to drain off their profits. But wealth was certainly attainable. Spanish millionaires, perhaps the best known being the Andalucian speculator José Salamanca, rose to dizzy heights of success. Some (like Salamanca) fell, others (like the

Spanish cartoon of Uncle Sam with his programme for the war, Admiral Sampson, who carried it out, and Paco, the Spanish soldier who brings the plans to naught.

Basque and Catalan industrialists) went on to found new trading empires. The break in this pattern of success came with the grave economic crisis of 1867.

The crisis forced many to re-examine the values by which their society lived. It was in these years that a group of Castilian professors turned from the French-dominated culture and economy to the apparently more independent thinking of a German philosopher called Krause. The growth of Krausism, as taught mainly by the Madrid Professor Sanz del Río (d. 1869), came to represent an intellectual revolt against the conservative forces in society, though in fact the Krausists had very modest aims. After the Revolution of 1868 some of them, notably Francisco Giner de los Ríos, set up the Free Institute of Education (1876), run by a group of Castilians who wanted Spain to look for knowledge and progress to Europe. Thanks to this movement the intellectuals began once again to play an active part in public life. Traditionalists, however, saw in them the introduction of alien ways of thought. The disaster of 1898 affected the intellectuals to an unprecedented degree. Schooled as many of them were in the outlook of Giner de los Ríos, they struck out at the weaknesses of a society which had nurtured itself on the illusion of empire. Joaquín Costa, perhaps the most practical-minded and least 'literary' of the 'generation

Painting by P. Junyent and Vilumara, two local 'scene' painters, of the industrial area of Barcelona, c. 1920.

Advertisement for the Colonial Company, offering ground coffee, teas and other colonial produce, and a textile factory in Barcelona, 1888.

141

View of the Gran Via in Madrid.

of '98', called for fundamental economic reforms. Other members of this 'generation' – they included the novelist Pio Baroja, the poet Antonio Machado, the essayist Ortega y Gasset, the philosopher Miguel de Unamuno – emerged not only as critics but as discoverers of a new richness in Spain's own cultural resources, in art, music and philosophy.

The early twentieth century saw a growth of the twin problems of regionalism and working-class agitation. Both were concentrated in Catalonia. As the economically most advanced area of Spain, Catalonia produced an active urban proletariat and a no less active business and intellectual élite. It consequently became the dominant centre of conflict in the early 1900s. The working-class problem between 1800 and 1930 is almost exclusively a Catalan one. Unions grew up in the province in the mid-nineteenth century, and foreign ideas, particularly those of the anarchist leader Bakunin, were disseminated from 1869 onwards. Initially strongest in rural Andalucia, anarchism was rapidly crushed there and moved on to strike roots in the Catalan labouring classes. In 1911 in Barcelona the greatest of the anarchist trade unions – the CNT (Confederación Nacional de Trabajo) – was born. The socialist movement, on the other hand, failed to implant itself firmly in Catalonia, and established its centre instead at Madrid, where it spoke not only for Castilian labourers but also for the workers

in the industrialized Basque provinces. It was in Madrid that the chief socialist trade union, the UGT (Union General de Trabajadores, founded in 1882), set up its headquarters. The difference between the two large workers' movements was not simply one of ideology: it was also, far more deeply, one of method. The socialists were committed to working for political power, and could be regarded as reformists; many anarchists, on the other hand, were wedded to the use of violence and the negation of all authority.

Life in the countryside was directly affected by population growth and its two most notable consequences: the expansion of towns, and an increase in overseas emigration. The cities and towns of modern Spain took shape in this period. Towns burst out of their medieval walls; squares were opened up; the streets were widened to take in the increased traffic of cycles and trams. Madrid's wide Gran Via belongs to this period, as does Barcelona's Via Layetana. Emigration began in the late nineteenth century and continued until the outbreak of the First World War. In the peak year, 1912, some 134,000 Spaniards left the peninsula to seek a new home in America. They augmented the 'Spanishness' of the New World, and strengthened commercial links with the American republics. Behind this picture of a population on the move lay an immense background of rural misery. From peasants with tiny plots too small for sustenance (as in

The first electric street-lighting in Madrid, on the Puerta del Sol.

Galicia, whence large numbers emigrated to America) to labourers who had no land at all (which was the general situation in Andalucia), the problem was one that none of the piecemeal attempts at reform had adequately attacked. Workers' organizations tended to press for a wholesale redistribution of land in order to break up the great *latifundia* and create an economically independent peasantry. In Andalucia in the early century some 1 per cent of landowners owned 42 per cent of the landed wealth. The labourers, known as *braceros*, went without work for perhaps one-third of the year. Redistribution by itself would not have solved these problems. Much of the land was not irrigated, the soil was loose and poorly planted, and the labourers themselves would not have had adequate money to invest in improvements. So the agrarian problem remained unsolved, and has continued to be a major difficulty for all twentieth-century governments. Agriculture, which makes up about a third of the national income and occupies nearly half the labour force, is the most backward sector in the country's economy. Rural unemployment was a major problem: in some Andalucian country towns the level in 1936 was as high as 50 per cent. The general result was that in both town and country the economic condition of the working population was little better in 1930 than it had been in 1830.

The rapid growth of industry side by side with the unmitigated backwardness of the rural economy, the impoverishment of the *braceros* together with an increase in town unemployment, the awakening of the intellectuals and the infiltration of new subversive ideas, combined to pose a wholly new problem for the government: the beginnings of mass agitation. Professional agitators like Bakunin's disciple Fanelli (in Spain in 1869) fed explosive situations with inflammatory doctrines. Early agrarian violence in Andalucia was followed by a convergence of the violent trends on Catalonia. In Barcelona bomb-throwing and convent-burning became the extremist reaction to police repression and torture. The trend culminated in the 'Tragic Week' (1909). A Catalan general strike degenerated for three days in July into an orgy of destruction: nearly fifty churches and convents in Barcelona were burned, nuns were raped, graves were dug up. Repression was merciless: troops were called in and hundreds of workers were shot.

It was difficult for the government to regain control of a rapidly deteriorating situation. In 1902 Alfonso XIII came of age and began to reign personally. Impatient of constitutional restrictions on his power, he withheld his confidence from most of the politicians. A series of conservative ministries, notably one under Antonio Maura, ruled until 1909, when the consequences of the 'Tragic Week' brought Maura down. Subsequent liberal ministries managed to pass some useful radical legislation with the help of republican deputies. The

Pablo Picasso, *The Blind Man's Meal* (1903), one of the Blue Period paintings from
Picasso's residence in Barcelona during the years 1900–4.

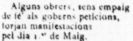
Alguns obrers, sens empaig
de fé als goberns peticions,
forjan manifestacions
pel dia 1.ª de Maig.

Y altres obrers delsíque creuhen
que pidolant res s'obté,
una huelga volen fe
per si més profit ne treuhen.

Y sens sabé' hont se decar
l'obrer en aquest ensaig,
arriba 'l 1.ª de Maig
del any mil vuytcents norat

focus of activity in Spanish politics was already moving away from the
cortes to the regions. The outbreak of a major economic and social
crisis in 1917, the very year of the Bolshevik Revolution, had profound effects on the country.

As a neutral, Spain had profited somewhat from the First World
War. By 1917 this success had evaporated. Groups of officers, supported by both republican and workers' parties, united against the
régime. In the summer, popular violence broke out, both in Madrid
(at Cuatro Caminos, where soldiers shot the strikers) and in Barcelona.
Regionalism came into its own: the Catalan leader Francisco Cambó
spoke out for the independent interests of Catalonia. A 'national
government' with Maura, Cambó and other conservatives attempted
with partial success to ward off revolution. When it fell, the initiative
returned to the two great forces that were to determine early twentieth-
century politics: the masses, and the army.

From 1917 to 1923 the labouring classes were fighting off a post-war
slump and general unemployment. Throughout eastern and southern
Spain there were revolutionary strikes in the country areas, many of
them quite successful. In 1919 in Barcelona the CNT carried out
what was probably its most impressive strike action, against the
Canadiense electricity company: the entire city was plunged into
darkness and brought virtually to a standstill. But employers retaliated
just as firmly, by the use of dismissals, lock-outs and police violence.
Anarchist ideologues used the weapon of assassination with increasing
frequency. But the violence spent itself, and many workers' organizations turned instead to support the more moderate UGT. The UGT,
together with its political wing, the socialist party under Largo
Caballero, thereupon became the single most powerful representative
of the Spanish working class. What the CNT's reign of terror had

a que no están per pamplinas
mpte acaban la paciencia,
:ordan la resistencia
amp de las Carolinas.

Y practicant lo acordat
aquella tarde mateixa,
la por ja comensa á creixe
per dintre'de la ciutat.

Los senyors ab la maleta,
pel que puga succehir,
desseguit se 'ls veu fugir
per sí 'ls feyan la traveta.

The turn of the nineteenth and twentieth centuries saw the growth of a working-class consciousness, especially strong in the industrial region of Catalonia.

Left, popular woodcuts of a 1 May demonstration in Barcelona.

Below, attack on general Martínez Campos during the anarchist bombings in Barcelona, September 1893.

unfortunately provoked was recourse by the employers and conservatives to military authority. This development was brought nearer by the Moroccan episode.

North Africa remained the last promising field for the exercise of Spanish military glory. For several years Spanish troops had been busy in Morocco keeping the tribesmen at bay. In 1921 the army was overwhelmed at its outpost of Anual, and in the hasty retreat lost some fourteen thousand men. The fortress of Melilla only narrowly escaped falling into the hands of the leader of the Rif tribesmen, Abd-el-Krim. The uproar created in Spain by revelations of the incompetence and corruption that made the disaster at Anual possible served to discredit the parliamentary régime. With the assured support of those who wanted effective, strong rule, the captain-general of Barcelona, General Primo de Rivera, 'pronounced' in September 1923 against the government.

The dictatorship (1923–30) was the last gasp of constitutional monarchy. Primo de Rivera's *coup* succeeded, as Raymond Carr says, 'because he caught parliamentary rule in its transition from oligarchy to democracy'. At the same time, his accession to power coincided with the acceptance of dictators in other countries such as Turkey and Italy. Though Primo was hostile to politicians and believed in the effectiveness of a salutary period of iron rule, he genuinely wished to hold power only temporarily, and then to hand the reins over to purified constitutional government.

A strong hand was undoubtedly required. Primo de Rivera settled the Moroccan question successfully. His ministers, notably

Sketch of the proceedings against a Catalan anarchist, 1908.

Calvo Sotelo, proposed important financial reforms. Progress was made in several major public schemes, particularly in irrigation. Though most political parties refused to co-operate actively, a section of the socialists collaborated in order to gain advantages for their unions. The experiment, however, attracted more and more enemies as it went on. The international financial crisis of 1929 made it impossible for some of his ministers to continue. Finally Primo lost the support of the army. He wrote a note to the generals asking for their support, but received prevaricating replies. In January 1930 he presented his resignation to the King and retired to Paris, where he died two months later.

By identifying himself for too long with the dictatorship, Alfonso XIII drew on himself the obloquy that Primo had earned. Leading politicians now declared themselves converted to the cause of a republic. An anti-monarchist committee consisting of liberals, radicals, regionalists and socialists planned measures to overthrow the

Spectators at a café concert: painting by Francisco Domingo (1894–).

government. An ill-timed *pronunciamiento* in December led to the
capture of the rebels and the execution of two officers. Their deaths, as
martyrs for the republic, were symbolically important. Several members
of the revolutionary committee were arrested. The government saw
that it would have to trust to public opinion. Plans for a general
election were rejected, and it was thought that municipal elections
would be easier to control. These were held on 12 April 1931. The
result was an overwhelming vote of support for the republicans and
the socialists. On 14 April Barcelona and San Sebastian declared the
Republic. A republican flag was hoisted over the telephone building
in central Madrid. The commander of the Civil Guard informed the
palace that he could not side with the government against the revolution. Alfonso's chief minister Romanones advised him to leave
Spain immediately. That evening, as the crowds massed in the square
before the palace, the King slipped out and took the road to the port
of Cartagena, where he caught a ship for Marseilles.

Left, General Miguel Primo de Rivera inspecting a military position in Morocco. Primo de Rivera's successful pacifica-tion of Spanish Morocco (he led the operations in person) was the greatest success of his régime.

Opposite, portrait of King Al-fonso XIII. The King's scorn for parliamentary government led him to welcome Primo de Rivera's dictatorship in 1923; when it fell, a strong upsurge of Republican feeling forced him to flee the country.

151

6

Modern Spain

The Second Republic, born amid mass enthusiasm in 1931, survived long enough to arouse the hopes of every sector of opinion and yet to disappoint them all. The constitution adopted by the new *cortes* was a model of progressive idealism. There was one chamber in parliament, which could be dissolved by the president of the Republic. Various rights were guaranteed, including the rights of the regions. But immediately problems arose with the article of the constitution separating Church and state. The struggle over religion, entered into by the Republic from the very beginning, was to become one of the major reasons for its eventual failure.

The Republic inherited all the reformist attitudes towards the Church that the old liberal tradition had professed. Catholicism had been so integral a part of the Spanish outlook, however, that no anti-clericals had dared to go beyond a few basic measures, such as those of 1836–37. Now the majority of the *cortes*, in the first flush of victory, demanded sweeping changes that would have severely hit the religious orders, stripped the Church of its property and schools, and reduced it to the same level as other faiths. One government minister, Manuel Azaña, proclaimed that 'Spain has ceased to be Catholic'. Then in May 1931 extremist groups began lightning incendiary attacks on churches and convents in Madrid. The agitation spread immediately to other towns and throughout Andalucia. Hundreds of major buildings were completely gutted. The crisis alienated Catholic opinion from the Republic, and caused a split in the government. The prime minister and the minister of the interior both resigned, and the Basque deputies seceded from the *cortes*.

The haste of the anti-clericals had equally unfruitful results in education. Article Twenty-Six forbade the religious orders to teach. This meant shutting primary schools, where some 600,000 pupils were being educated. Yet the state had no means of building or staffing schools to replace those closed down. Criticisms of the Republic are relatively easy to make in retrospect. The ministers were often aware of the dangers they faced. But men such as Azaña were adamant that only a firm stand would win through. In the event, lack of experience and underestimation of the difficulties were obstacles too great to be overcome by firmness alone.

This bronze statue of a mother and her children, riddled with bullets during the battle for Madrid, recalls the savagery of the Civil War and the deep splits in Spanish society that caused it.

The Republic was not afraid to face problems squarely. The issue of Catalonia was solved by granting the Catalans a Statute that gave them effective autonomy. A Statute was prepared for the Basques. But the real problems arose in the social field. How were the workers and peasants, who were the backbone of support for the Republic, to be appeased? Centuries of social injustice, it was soon found, could not be cured in a day.

The agrarian problem was one the Republic had committed itself to solving. But the variety of solutions proposed merely reflected the variety of political complexions that made up the government. The Marxists demanded a total expropriation of the land. Moderate

socialists felt that so radical a programme would doom the Republic, and a socialist in the *cortes* reassured the public that 'the agrarian reform is not directed against the régime of private property'. The agrarian legislation passed in 1932 turned out to be extremely disappointing. It catered for central and southern Spain only. By the end of 1933 the government had resettled less than ten thousand landless families, and had taken over only about ninety thousand hectares. The socialist leader Largo Caballero sourly and perhaps reasonably called this legislation 'an aspirin to cure an appendicitis'. Agrarian unrest continued at an advanced pace. In Andalucia the anarchists agitated against the failure of the socialists in Madrid to accelerate reform. Two

Virulent anti-clericalism came to the fore in the Republic of 1931. *Opposite*, the destruction of a church in Catalonia; *above*, a Carmelite nun is led from a burning convent.

incidents in particular showed the savagery of the mood in rural areas. In 1932 in the little village of Castilblanco (Extremadura province) four civil guards were killed in a riot and their bodies mutilated. A year later in the Andalucian village of Casas Viejas a group of anarchists staged a pathetic little rising; the government called in troops and planes, and twenty-five villagers were shot, many in cold blood. Casas Viejas discredited the Azaña government: here were socialists brutally repressing common people just as in the days before the Republic. The agrarian masses, shocked, swung round to oppose the government. In this they were joined by the working classes.

As minister of labour, Largo Caballero instituted a great volume of progressive legislation to help the working man. Minimum wages and an eight-hour day became law. The UGT, the socialist union, co-operated with government policy. But bitter opposition to government tactics came from the anarchist CNT and its political wing the FAI (Federación Anarquista Ibérica), which had its stronghold in industrial Catalonia. They organized strikes and revolts against the Republican authorities. In Seville in July 1931 a strike was put down by the authorities: thirty people were killed, three hundred wounded. In Catalonia risings on a more ambitious scale were attempted, all unsuccessfully. On each occasion the working classes were encouraged to identify repressive action with the Republic.

The most fundamental reason for these disheartening events was simple bad luck: the Republic had come into being in the middle of a world economic slump. The government was unable to promote any serious reforms because it had no money. The country was suffering widespread unemployment, and no system of unemployment benefit was in existence. Meanwhile, political opposition was growing. Army officers felt their loyalties (usually monarchist and Catholic) sorely tried, Carlists began collecting arms, on the left the tiny communist party was blossoming. The most important constitutional group to emerge on the right was the CEDA (Confederación de Derechas Autónomas), led by the brilliant young lawyer Gil Robles. Originally a movement with leanings towards the right-wing régimes in Italy and Germany, the CEDA settled down to become the party of constitutional Catholicism. More overtly fascist groups grew up at this time. In Valladolid the JONS (Juntas de Ofensiva Nacional Sindicalista), inspired by Onésimo Redondo, took as its symbol the yoke and arrows emblem of the Catholic Monarchs; in Madrid, José Antonio Primo de Rivera, son of the dictator, founded the strongly apolitical and apocalyptic Falange. Each of these groups found ready support in a country where the government seemed to have failed. The Casas Viejas affair finally put an end to Azaña's coalition. The prisons were full, unemployment was rife, police were everywhere.

Opposite, Civil Guards making an arrest in Madrid, 1933, and, *beneath*, the massacre at Casas Viejas.

Elections in 1933 turned out the government and brought in the parties of the centre, mainly the CEDA and the radicals. The latter group was entrusted with the government. The Republic survived, but moved rightwards.

The next two years are commonly known as the *bienio negro*, the two black years. Under the new government virtually all the legislation of the previous administration was undone, and the rights of property and of the Church reaffirmed. The progressive parties had not in fact lost their hold on the electorate; their defeat can be attributed largely to the complex electoral law and to internal dissensions. Faced by a reactionary government, the anarchists resorted to direct and open revolution. A premature attempt at a rising in Saragossa at the end of 1933 was followed by a wave of anarchist-inspired strikes throughout Spain. The impatience of working people was brought home to the socialist UGT, which now followed Largo Caballero in switching from constitutionalist to revolutionary tactics. In February 1934, Caballero stated that 'the only hope of the masses is now in social revolution'. An attempt was made to unite the various workers' movements, but the anarchists in particular refused to co-operate. At the same time social conditions were deteriorating rapidly as unemployment soared.

The central government then fell foul of the regionalist parties in Catalonia and Biscay. The Catalan leftist party, led by Luis Companys, resented central interference in Catalan legislation. The Basques demanded a Statute of Autonomy. A further danger threatened from the right: the CEDA demanded a majority position in the Cabinet. The left opposition issued threats against any move to take the CEDA into the government. As a compromise the radical prime minister accepted three lesser CEDA figures into the Cabinet. One historian has commented that 'all the disasters that have followed for Spain may be traced to this one unhappy decision'. On the next day, 5 October 1934, the socialist UGT called a nation-wide strike in protest. Republicans of all shades, including conservatives, boycotted the government. Major revolutionary uprising broke out across the country.

In Catalonia, Companys on 6 October declared the independence of 'the Catalan state within the Federal Republic'. Unsupported by the anarchists, this *coup* collapsed. The army surrounded the municipal building and arrested Companys. An attempt at a socialist rising in Madrid was likewise crushed. But in the mining districts of Asturias a wholly different battle was fought. On 5 October the various workers' movements united to support a rising of miners who stormed a police station and then began to take over the regional capital, Oviedo. This mass rising was successful for a while. But within a fortnight it had been ruthlessly crushed by legionaries and Moorish troops rushed in from Africa: the toll was over two thousand dead, twice as many wounded. The brutal repression was directed from Madrid by General Francisco Franco.

In the wake of these revolutionary events nearly every prominent leftist leader was arrested and imprisoned. A reshuffle of the administration made it more right-wing and acceptable to the propertied classes. It proved impossible, however, to eliminate the leftist leaders, because of popular reaction against the excessive brutality in Asturias. The leaders emerged from prison in a militant mood. The reactionary agrarian policies of the government coalition alienated the great mass of rural unemployed, while the urban workers were roused by the heroic symbolism of the Asturias uprising. Government scandals (one of these, the *straperlo* affair, gave Spanish its word for black-marketeering),

Maps showing the course of the Civil War.

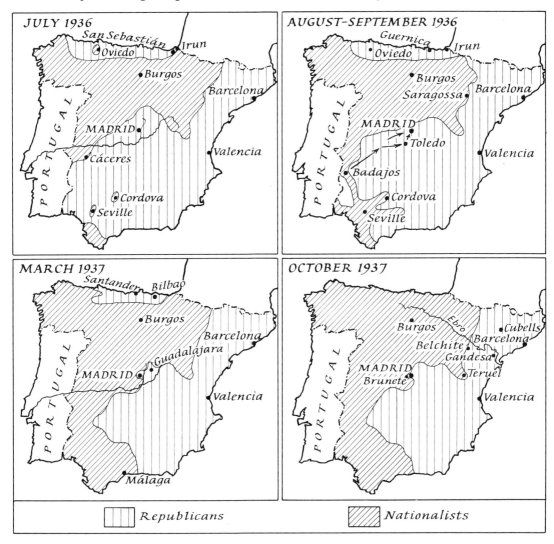

JULY 1936 · San Sebastián · Irun · Oviedo · Burgos · Barcelona · PORTUGAL · MADRID · Cáceres · Valencia · Cordova · Seville

AUGUST-SEPTEMBER 1936 · Guernica · Irun · Oviedo · Burgos · Saragossa · Barcelona · MADRID · Toledo · PORTUGAL · Badajos · Cordova · Valencia · Seville

MARCH 1937 · Santander · Bilbao · Burgos · Barcelona · Guadalajara · PORTUGAL · MADRID · Valencia · Málaga

OCTOBER 1937 · Burgos · Ebro · Cubells · Belchite · Barcelona · Gandesa · PORTUGAL · MADRID · Teruel · Brunete · Valencia

⊓⊓⊓ *Republicans*   ⧄ *Nationalists*

General Franco (centre), com/mander of the Nationalist forces, entering Burgos, the insurgent capital; on his left is General Mola, chief planner of the *pronunciamiento*.

and widespread distrust of Gil Robles, won further support for the left. A 'Popular Front' including all leftist parties, even the anarchists, was formed. When the elections took place in February 1936, the Front, though it attracted barely half the national vote, won two/thirds of the seats in the *cortes*. The right wing had been crushed by its own electoral law.

The triumphant Republicans, led by Azaña, claimed that 'we are moderate'. Power remained in Republican hands right down to the generals' rising in July, and no socialists took part in the govern/ment. Yet the initiative had really passed from both the *cortes* and the Republicans. In the streets and the countryside it was the factions and the populace that took over. Rightist support swung from the de/feated parliamentarians to the extra/parliamentary Falange and the army. On the left the communist party, drawing on Russian goodwill, began to grow. Fascist terrorists beat up and murdered opponents with impunity. Leftists burned churches and killed civil guards. A helpless government watched as popular movements took the law into their own hands: peasants seized land and expelled landlords. Alarmed by the clear threat to property and order, the army began

consultations with right-wing politicians. Calvo Sotelo, the former finance minister during the dictatorship, assumed leadership of the plotters. On 12 July he was assassinated by some police officers as reprisal for a murder committed by the Falangists. The horrified generals brought the date of the planned uprising forward, and on 17 July the army in Morocco, commanded by Francisco Franco, 'pronounced'. On 18 July the rising became general throughout all Spanish military garrisons.

Never Sated. Drawing by André Masson satirizing the Church's support of the Nationalist cause.

The generals leading the plot – Mola, Franco, Goded – expected a swift, efficient take-over. But the army now had to reckon not with helpless politicians but with popular masses which, experienced in militant action, could not easily be crushed. The rebellion crumbled where armed workers took to the streets: the failure of Goded in Barcelona was the most notable. Several factors therefore combined to make the rising of 18 July emerge not merely as another *coup* but as the opening of a long, bitter civil war which in its essentials has not even today come to an end.

The rebels claimed to speak for Spain, but tended rather to represent only its traditionalist side. Enemies of the Republic such as Carlists and monarchists, the majority of the clergy, Falangists, were prominent on the side of the army. The government drew its strength principally from the parties on the left, the socialists and anarchists, and from the invaluable help of the Catalans and Basques, who had both been granted autonomy within the Republic. Most of all, the government could rely on the common people, who effectively formed the backbone of resistance to the rebel army. In July 1936 the Nationalist side, as the rebels were called, had managed to secure some important cities in Andalucia and the greater part of Old Castile and Aragon. These gains were made only after a great deal of bloodshed, by the wholesale massacre of dissidents in areas that were afterwards claimed to be purely Nationalist. The crisis triggered off an orgy of destruction and bloodshed throughout Spain. Enraged Republicans and anti-clericals took vengeance on members of the upper classes and on the Church. Church buildings were gutted, archives destroyed, and nearly five thousand clergy killed in cold blood. The extremism of this fratricide meant that by 1937 most Spaniards had, if only to protect themselves, been pushed into one camp or the other. Many were compelled to adopt a side simply because they were there when events happened. Some, like the poet García Lorca (shot by Nationalists in 1936), were killed for unknown reasons and their bodies hurled into unidentified graves.

For three brutal years the two Spains grappled with each other. Heroism, such as that of the besieged in the Nationalist-held Alcázar of Toledo or in the streets of Republican Madrid, was morally overshadowed by the gratuitous and often typically Spanish cruelty of the conflict. It was a civil war that cost well over half a million lives, and immeasurable material damage. Many people simplified the struggle as being a crusade against communism or, alternatively, a war against fascism. The issues were inevitably more complex. It was the intensely Catholic Basques, for instance, who stood firmly by the anti-clerical Republic. And it was they who were among the first to be mown down from the air by the professed defenders of Christian civilization. In April 1937, in the market-town of Guernica, before whose historic oak tree the liberties of the Basques were traditionally sworn to by the Crown, flights of German bombers flew over regularly for a period of three hours and flattened the town centre. Over 1,600 people were killed, 900 wounded. We can visualize the impact on world opinion through the canvas which the Catalan artist Picasso, then in France, dedicated to the event.

The war was seen as a great ideological issue both by foreign leftists fighting for the Republic (the International Brigades contributed significantly to the war effort) and by foreign Catholics on the Franco side. The great totalitarian powers intervened with money, men and

Detail of *Guernica* by Picasso.

P.S.U.

FEIXISME NO!

arms. The Soviet Union extended limited aid to the Republic, but pressed secretly for control over policy-making. The government shipped its gold reserves out to Russia, where they were all used up in the purchase of weapons for Spain. The Germans and Italians intervened more seriously and in the long run more effectively. German tanks and planes served to turn the balance of the war against the government. The Western democracies stood idly by in the name of a policy of 'non-intervention'.

The Republican government moved from crisis to crisis without ever attaining stability. Deprived in July 1936 of almost half the country, of the biggest grain-producing areas, of most of the army and generals, of most of the Civil Guard and police, it had to adopt makeshift solutions. The support of the masses was not enough; it remained none the less, as the heroic defence of Madrid showed, the greatest strength of the régime. The Republic would have collapsed within months but for the material help given by the Soviet Union. Policy differences within the Republic proved to be one of its great weaknesses, and the importation of Soviet police methods was wholly unpalatable to many of the leaders, notably the socialist prime minister, Largo Caballero. The extermination by the Russians of the

Quel héroisme! One of a series of lithographs by Morère of the siege of Irún, September 1936.

Fascism No! Poster issued by the Catalan Socialist Party.

Sketch of a Nationalist officer during the operations on the northern front.

leaders of dissident Catalan communists of the POUM was typical of the internecine strife within Republican ranks. By 1939 the widely resented domination of the communists (Negrín, the Republic's last premier, was their nominee), and policy splits between anarchists and socialists, had led to a collapse of authority.

The Nationalists benefited almost from the first from a united command. The death by accident of Franco's two rivals for leadership, Generals Sanjurjo and Mola, and the murder in a Republican prison at Alicante in 1936 of José Antonio Primo de Rivera, left Franco in sole charge. In 1937 he was proclaimed leader (*caudillo*) of Spain, and chief of state. In the course of the war the various alliances which went to make up Nationalist Spain were elaborated. The extreme monarchism of the Carlists and the social fascism of the Falangists were both soon repressed by being fused in 1937 into a single party, the only one ever permitted in the Nationalist state. This was the clumsily titled 'FET y de las JONS' (the FET stood for Falange Española Tradicionalista), known for short as the Movement (*el Movimiento*). The basic strength of the Nationalist coalition lay in its counter-revolutionary stand for a traditionalist Spain. The Germans were never allowed to dominate Franco, who accepted their advice and munitions but subsequently refused to enter the European war on Hitler's side.

The suffering caused by the war to all social classes was immense. But it also aroused intense idealism and enthusiasm. On the Nationalist side the adoption of a visionary rhetoric borrowed from José Antonio gave ideological respectability to the cause; it also fired the spirits of young militants fighting for an 'authentic' Spain free from pollution by foreign influences such as Marxism, Judaism and Freemasonry. The achievements of Germany and Italy aroused a grateful enthusiasm for fascism, and the fascist salute became so common in Francoist Spain that even bishops were seen to give it. The idea of a 'crusade' against communism received the official blessing of the Church (after the events of 1936, most clergy had good reason for hostility to the Republic), and a familiar term for the civil war was for long simply 'the crusade'.

An outstanding feature of the Republican side was the almost unanimous sympathy of Spanish intellectuals for it, from García Lorca, murdered in 1936 at Granada, to Antonio Machado, who died just across the French border in 1939 as a refugee from his martyred country. The victory of the Nationalists meant the voluntary exile from Spain of every significant progressive thinker, poet and artist. A whole generation of talent went abroad (chiefly to France and Latin America) in protest: among them were the poets Rafael Alberti and Juan Ramón Jiménez, the musician Pau Casals, the film director Buñuel, the historians Américo Castro and Sánchez Albornoz. In

Ceremonial parade held by the Falange in Barcelona at the end of the Civil War.

the war many of the intellectuals contributed by writing songs and ballads when they were not actually fighting. Popular culture found a new voice. This too was part of the real, 'authentic' Spain.

The war ended in March 1939 with the fall of Madrid after its military commander had revolted against the communist-dominated government. The victors were in no mood for mercy. Republican sympathizers were exterminated in mass executions: in Madrid over a thousand death sentences a month were passed. It has been conserva-tively estimated that as many people were put to death by the winning side *after* the war as had been executed by both sides together during the three years of conflict. Between 1939 and 1942 some two millions passed through the Nationalist prisons. It was a ferocious ending to a ferocious war. Over 600,000 people had died in battle or by assassi-nation during the three years. Recovery was to be slow, for the end of the Spanish struggle coincided with the opening of the Second World War. In one sense, the wounds were never to be healed. The Nationalist victory was a partisan one of half Spain over the other half. Concilia-tion was not attempted. In Catalonia autonomy was completely abolished and official use of Catalan forbidden. Basque independence likewise disappeared. The government remained, and remains, wedded to a traditionalist and anti-democratic viewpoint alien to that held by the supporters of the Republic. For reasons of this type, the fall of the Republic in 1939 was simply the end of the armed phase of struggle. The basic disagreement among Spaniards, over ideology and social policy, still continues.

During the Second World War, Franco managed to keep Spain neutral. The public attitude of the government remained pro-Axis, a Germanophile (Franco's brother-in-law Serrano Suñer) became foreign minister, and a specially recruited force, the Blue Division, was sent to fight on the Eastern Front against the Russians. But the Caudillo's habitual caution made him stop short of direct intervention on Germany's side. He met Hitler in 1940 on the frontier at Hendaya and reaffirmed his neutrality. In the early years of the war the Press rejoiced at German victories. By 1944 a change in tone had taken place. The régime made itself out to be less pro-nazi than anti-communist. This was to be the winning tune. In 1944 one of the leaders of Catholic Action, Martín Artajo, became foreign minister. The government, it was impressed on the Allies, was committed to the defence of Western culture against Bolshevism. Between 1945 and 1948, when the Cold War reached its height, Spain came to be seen by America as a likely ally in the struggle against Soviet domination.

After peace in 1945, Spain was universally boycotted as a fascist power and excluded from the United Nations. Its political and strategic value in the anti-communist West was soon appreciated,

Poster issued by the Republic for distribution in France. The caption reads: 'The "military" action of the rebels. Europe tolerates and defends it. Your children can expect it' – a prophecy that was soon to be fulfilled during the Second World War.

however, and several countries opened diplomatic links. Then in 1950 the United States granted a large loan to Franco and also appointed an ambassador. From this point onwards the régime consolidated its position in the international community. Its most successful year was probably 1953, when an agreement on the loan of military bases was signed with America: Spain was to receive $226,000,000 in aid. In the same year a Concordat was signed with the Vatican. All the Western countries now had diplomatic links with Spain. The régime had become respectable. In 1955 the country was accepted as a member of the United Nations.

The big struggle to restore the country's economy took some time to gather momentum. Agriculture, still one of the most important sectors of the economy, remains backward. Agrarian produce accounts for one-fifth of Spain's wealth and half its exports; it also occupies, on the average, one-third of the working population. Various reforms have been put into effect, the most successful being the redistribution and consolidation of peasant smallholdings. Big new irrigation schemes have been introduced. But progress has been limited, and agricultural growth very slow. Production per producer actually *fell* between 1930 and 1957. The government has been unwilling to take any radical measures over what are essentially social problems, such as the reform of the great private estates or the low level of agricultural wages. Rural unemployment is a major problem which in the late 1950s and early 1960s led the government to allow over a million impoverished labourers to emigrate – without their families – to Germany and other countries in order to earn a living. The general picture, conceded by official statistics, is one of stagnation. The agrarian problem remains, as it always has been, a major blight on the country.

Industry, on the other hand, has advanced rapidly. The heavy industries of Catalonia and Cantabria now have offshoots in other parts of the country, where the government has designated special growth areas. Foreign investment has played an important part in the industrial boom, by far the largest sums consisting of American money, both from official sources (a direct aid programme began in 1954) and from private investors. German, French and British investments are also substantial. A visitor to Spain today will find that many articles he buys – whether a car (the Spanish 'Seat' is made under licence from Italy's 'Fiat') or aspirins (invariably manufactured by German chemical firms) – have foreign expertise and capital behind them. The difficulty in assessing Spain's industrial progress, however, lies in its unbalanced character. *Per capita* output in many key sectors (such as steel and electricity) is still fairly low. By contrast, luxury sectors have been allowed virtually uncontrolled growth: production

Two symbols representing the two chief bulwarks of Franco's Spain: the Cross, and the yoke and arrows, emblem of the Falange.

The port at Barcelona, through which the products of Catalonia's booming industries are exported.

of cars between 1963 and 1967 nearly quadrupled, the building industry has almost choked itself by over-expansion. The important tourist industry, which occupies a large proportion of the nation's labour force, has boosted the national income but made little impact on real growth. Official figures can thus truthfully point to an advancing economy, but it is an economy in which there is considerable disequilibrium. The most notable consequence has been a rapid increase in inflation: in 1971–72 the rise was of the order of 10 per cent. The average wages of the working population have not kept pace with this fall in living standards, as social advisers have pointed out to the government. The gap between rich and poor remains as wide as ever, regardless of the official figures for industrial progress.

In the past two decades it has become clear that, long and peacefully as the present régime has maintained itself, it has been no more successful than its predecessors in solving the classic problems of Spanish history. The one great achievement has been over thirty years of peace.

Despite the 'peace', the spirit of discord has never been exorcized.

Ideological discord is the most widespread. The official teachings of the state have since 1937 been associated with 'the Movement', a name applied, as we have seen, to the union of Falangist and other tradi-tionalist elements under Franco. In recent years, Franco has shed his close ties with the Falangists and moved to ally with the Catholics and more recently with the technocrats. 'The Movement' still remains the only permitted outlook, and official pronouncements always pay lip-service to it; ritualistic appeals to 'Spain – One, United, Free' are the order of the day. But Falangist disillusion with Franco is now deep-rooted, and outbursts and riots on the part of Falangist youths are common. Holders of senior office in the state have to swear allegiance to the principles of the Movement, but it would seem that many do so with extensive mental reservations. While the ideological character of the régime may have weakened, its general tone is still there: in the massive official architecture, the indifference to democratic values, the rigidly middle-class nature of all public life, the close identification with clericalism, the obsession with sixteenth-century history, the permanence of the military spirit.

In political terms, the discord is obvious. Modern Spain is by no means a fascist state. Despite all the liberalization that has taken place, however, it is still a firmly authoritarian state. The press is controlled, and journalists have experienced exceptional difficulties with a press law of 1966 which theoretically abolished censorship. Newspapers erring on the side of boldness can find themselves put out of business (the liberal paper *Madrid* perished in this way in 1971). There is no political life, and though dissident groups exist they are tolerated only so that the police can keep an eye on them. Should they emerge into the open, as they did in 1962 when representatives of several parties attended a conference at Munich on the European Community, serious counter-measures are taken, including detention and exile. Opposition of any sort is rigidly repressed. Several hundred political prisoners appear to be detained in prisons at Burgos and elsewhere, but on the whole the government does not rely on incarceration as a means of silencing opponents. Executions are rare: the régime was clearly shaken by the world-wide revulsion against the execution in 1963 of Julián Grimau for alleged crimes committed a quarter of a century earlier. Some semblance of consultation and constitutional government exists in the *cortes*, which is not a parliament so much as a group of hand-picked men (they are called *procuradores*, a sixteenth-century term, to eliminate any idea that they are representative deputies). Less than one-fifth of the 565 members of the *cortes*, accord-ing to the terms of the Organic Law of 1966, are actually elected by the people; and even *they* are elected not by universal suffrage but by the

votes of heads of families alone. Democratic government, then, does not exist in Spain. Moreover, the overwhelming majority of the *procuradores* are wealthy, propertied members of the upper middle class. There is clearly a gap between the outlook and social status of the government and the governed.

Real power in any case does not rest with the constitutional bodies. Spain is still a dictatorship, and the head of state has sweeping powers. Technically, the country is still under military rule. Virtually all dissidents are tried by military tribunals on charges of 'military rebellion', a term which is defined so widely as to include every possible political act, from participating in strikes to being present at an unauthorized meeting or distributing an unlicensed pamphlet. The army remains the one fundamental pillar of the régime. The youth of Spain is imbued with official ideals by an obligatory period of military service. One result is the existence of a huge army that absorbs up to 40 per cent of the national budget. Since Spain has almost no external commitments and has been at peace internally since 1939, critics are able to categorize the army as a massive unproductive sector whose only function is the protection of the régime. Military service tends to relieve unemployment, but soldiers' wages have not been high and also suffer from inflation.

The middle class is the other main buttress of Franco's Spain. It is the prosperous businessman who is the best advertisement for the

A monarchy without a sovereign, Franco's Spain is obsessed with the military glory of the Reconquest and the Empire. *Opposite*, General Franco with Prince Juan, Alfonso XIII's heir; his son has been designated the Caudillo's successor. *Above*, march-past during the 1971 parade commemorating the end of the Civil War.

régime's success. Immense new banks in the middle of the capital cities proclaim an impressive growth in capital turnover and a great surge of confidence in the régime. Not all the financiers share this confidence: the government has uncovered several remarkable instances where prominent businessmen have illegally deposited their assets in Switzerland. But the ordinary middle-class man in the street is undoubtedly better housed and fed than he was a generation ago. The high degree of urban prosperity contrasts strangely with the under-developed state of the villages in the countryside. This again is a re-minder of the imbalance in the Spanish achievement. Consumer luxuries, cars and television sets, are booming: all are symbols of the middle-class emphasis of Spanish capitalism. The annual deluge of tourists reinforces this emphasis: there were 500,000 foreign visitors to Spain in 1950, twenty years later there were twenty million. All the luxury service industries are geared to meeting the needs of this highly profitable source of foreign exchange.

For long looked upon as the bulwark of the régime, the Church is now searching for a new role. The modern Catholic Church in Spain is no longer the wealthy institution it used to be: governments from 1835 to 1939 have seen to that. It has had a pre-eminently privileged position since 1939: freedom from much taxation, the virtual monopoly of primary and secondary education, the sole validity of Church marriage, public recognition of only one religion. Ecclesiastical authority has dominated many spheres of secular life, notably university education and censorship of the creative arts. Since the 1950s, however, there has been a remarkable change in Church attitudes. While Catholics in high public positions have co-operated closely as ministers in the government, either through Catholic Action or through the more recently active lay group 'Opus Dei', the lower ranks of Catholic Action, in particular the HOAC Workers' Brotherhoods (Hermandades Obreras de Acción Catolica), have adopted a more critical attitude to Church-state relations. The main reason for rethinking has been the realization that despite the Church's privileged position, or perhaps because of it, the level of Catholic belief has sunk alarmingly low. Azaña's claim that 'Spain has ceased to be Catholic' has been confirmed by various surveys. In 1950 the Archbishop of Valencia estimated that only 17 per cent of the popu-lation of his diocese were practising Catholics: 'the great mass of the workers does not love the Church', was his opinion. A survey made in 1959 in a Madrid suburb showed that no more than 35 per cent of the population, virtually all of them middle-class, were churchgoers. The alienation of the working class from religion in Barcelona is reflected in church attendance figures there of under 3 per cent. In other more staunchly Catholic parts of the country attendance is very

Street scene in Valencia, a characteristic juxtaposition of the primitive and modern ways of life in contemporary Spain.

much higher, but the general picture is still disturbing enough for Church leaders.

The Second Vatican Council and the encyclicals of Pope John XXIII have given progressive clergy the encouragement they need. The Basque priests have been particularly active, as in 1960 when 339 of them signed a letter containing a sweeping indictment of the régime. Basing themselves on papal pronouncements, some bishops have also contributed to the new face of the Spanish Church. Demands have been made by clergy for an end to the Concordat, a lifting of censorship, increases of up to 50 per cent in workers' basic wages, the recognition of the right of free association for workers and students, and so on. Priests have been arrested for subversion and given stiff sentences. Thanks in great part to the privileged position accorded it by the régime, the Church is well placed to provide a moral alternative for opponents of the existing system, and could prove to be a serious threat to its stability.

Opposition, if it is to be successful, could begin in one of the three foregoing pillars of the régime. The working class has been too deprived of political activity for it to be immediately effective. The continuity of strike action, in a country where strikes are wholly illegal, is nevertheless some guide to the hidden strength of the workers. The first great outburst of strikes since the Civil War occurred in 1962, mainly among the miners of Asturias, whence it spread to other parts of the country, until an estimated total of 150,000 men were on strike. In the late 1960s strike action was resorted to with great frequency by workers in a variety of callings, not only in heavy industry but even in state enterprises like the metro in Madrid. Despite this activity, and sporadic acts of terror carried out by organizations like the Basque separatist party ETA (Euzkadi Ta Askatatuna – Basque Land and Freedom), no serious threat to the government has been posed by the working class.

The story of student disorder is different. In the early sixties student discontent at their state-run unions led to demands for more democratic and representative bodies. While this has remained the basic reason for complaint, conflict has in fact broadened itself to involve such matters as civil liberty, police brutality and university autonomy from the state. The year 1968 produced serious conflicts in Spain as in France. Since then every year has witnessed protests, dismissals of staff and closures of faculties. This revolt of the children of the privileged classes has been too serious a threat to ignore, for many middle-class parents have come to sympathize with their children. University rectors have been sacked, statutes remodelled, police have been given extraordinary powers on campus, students have been shot; the germ of rebellion still remains. Intellectual youth is unable to accept a system

Juan Genovés, *Double Image*, 1966.

Spain's official image: poster issued by the Spanish Government Tourist Board, 1973.

where only lip-service is given to principles that the textbooks and laws guarantee.

Change is inevitable. Government policy since 1962 has concentrated single-mindedly on getting Spain accepted as a partner in the European Economic Community, which already takes over one-third of its foreign trade. In the process, the government has had to prove its acceptability by relaxing some of its attitudes. Free interchange with foreign countries, above all through tourism, has meant the importation of much of the commercial vulgarity of Western capitalism, but also of some of its more fruitful ideas. In many spheres – in scientific research, in theology, in political economy, and above all in the creative arts such as film/making – there has correspondingly been an impatience with the burden of traditionalism and an impetus to think freshly. The cultural poverty of the earlier years of the Franco régime, aggravated by the emigration of talent and the imposition of a heavy/handed censorship, is being succeeded by a more tolerant attitude to the arts. The obstacles to free development none the less remain substantial.

Despite many internal weaknesses, Spain is a strong country inter/nationally. It received wide support in 1965 for its confrontation with Great Britain over Gibraltar, a territory which is indubitably Spanish but where the inhabitants prefer British sovereignty. Formerly a protégé of the United States, the country has now adopted a more independent line, particularly in respect of the American bases on its soil. The régime's professed anti/communism is in sharp contrast to the close trade and cultural links it maintains with Cuba. Elsewhere in Latin America, it is at pains to keep up the ethnic and cultural bonds it associates with *Hispanidad*, that is, the 'Spanishness' of the former colonies. Recently it has signed commercial agreements with the major countries of eastern Europe, an important step towards establishing normal relations with the communist bloc.

Franco, indifferent to small murmurs of rebellion, plans for the future. The state has been technically a monarchy since its inception, with Franco as temporary guardian. In the long run the Caudillo certainly plans a restoration in the shape of Juan Carlos, son of the present Bourbon pretender, who has been groomed carefully for the task of becoming his successor and who in 1969 was recognized by the *cortes* as Prince of Spain. But no firm date for a restoration has been given. Ironically, it appears that the return of a constitutional monarchy might well be acceptable to a broad spectrum of the opposition. Spain is not a totalitarian state, and the machinery of government will not grind on unperturbed when Franco disappears from the scene. The question is whether changes can occur peacefully.

The problems of Spain are of long standing and not necessarily soluble in terms only of Western or of communist democracy. If changes occur freely, they will be in conformity with the remarkable humanity and genius of a nation that has yet to display its modern potential.

Suggestions for further reading

Paperback editions are marked with an asterisk.

BACKGROUND AND GENERAL
Stephen Clissold, *Spain* (London 1969)
R. Menéndez Pidal, *The Spaniards in their History* (London 1950)
* J.B. Trend, *The Civilization of Spain* (London 1967)
Miguel de Unamuno, *Invertebrate Spain* (London 1937)
Pierre Vilar, *Spain: a Brief History* (Oxford 1967)
J. Vicens Vives, *An Economic History of Spain* (Princeton 1969)

TRAVEL
The Blue Guide to Northern Spain
The Blue Guide to Southern Spain
George Borrow, *The Bible in Spain* (1843; Everyman edition 1961)
Gerald Brenan, *South from Granada* (London 1957)
Richard Ford, *Handbook for Travellers in Spain and Readers at Home*
    (1845; reissued in 3 vols, London 1966)
Julian Pitt-Rivers, *The people of the Sierra* (London 1954). A modern
    sociological study
Walter Starkie, *The Road to Santiago* (London 1957)

ART AND LITERATURE
Bernard Bevan, *History of Spanish Architecture* (London 1938)
* Gerald Brenan, *The Literature of the Spanish People* (Harmondsworth
    1963)
* J.M. Cohen (ed.), *The Penguin Book of Spanish Verse* (Harmondsworth
    1956)
Angel Fiores (ed.), *Spanish Drama* (New York 1962). Translations of
    plays
Otis H. Green, *Spain and the Western Tradition* (4 vols, Madison
    1963–66)
José Gudiol, *The Arts of Spain* (London 1964)
George Kubler and Martin Soria, *Art and Architecture in Spain and
    Portugal and their American Dominions 1500–1800* (Harmondsworth
    1959)
Jacques Lassaigne, *Spanish Painting from the Catalan Frescoes to El
    Greco* (Geneva 1962)

N. D. Shergold, *A History of the Spanish Stage* (Oxford 1967)
Enrique Sordo, *Moorish Spain* (London 1963)

ANCIENT AND MEDIEVAL SPAIN
The Cambridge Ancient History, vols 7–11 (Cambridge 1926–36)
Américo Castro, *The Structure of Spanish History* (Princeton 1954)
* Gabriel Jackson, *The Making of Medieval Spain* (London 1972)
H. C. Lea, *The Moriscos of Spain* (Philadelphia 1901)
R. Menéndez Pidal, *The Cid and his Spain* (London 1934)
W. Montgomery Watt, *A History of Islamic Spain* (Edinburgh 1965)
A. A. Neuman, *The Jews in Spain: their social, political and cultural life during the Middle Ages* (2 vols, Philadelphia 1944)

EARLY MODERN SPAIN
Fernand Braudel, *The Mediterranean and the Mediterranean World in the Age of Philip II*, vol. 1 (London 1972)
Antonio Domínguez Ortiz, *The Golden Age of Spain* (London 1971)
* J. H. Elliott, *Imperial Spain 1469–1716* (Harmondsworth 1970)
* Richard Herr, *The Eighteenth-Century Revolution in Spain* (Princeton 1970)
* Henry Kamen, *The Spanish Inquisition* (New York 1968)
* G. Mattingly, *The Defeat of the Spanish Armada* (London 1970)
* J. H. Parry, *The Spanish Seaborne Empire* (Harmondsworth 1973)

MODERN SPAIN
* Gerald Brenan, *The Spanish Labyrinth* (Harmondsworth 1960)
Pierre Broué and Emile Témime, *The Revolution and the Civil War in Spain* (London 1970)
Raymond Carr, *Spain 1808–1939* (Oxford 1966)
Brian Crozier, *Franco. A biographical history* (London 1967)
* Ernest Hemingway, *For Whom the Bell Tolls* (Harmondsworth 1969)
C. A. M. Hennessy, *The Federal Republic in Spain* (Oxford 1962)
* Gabriel Jackson, *The Spanish Republic and the Civil War* (Princeton 1968)
* George Orwell, *Homage to Catalonia* (Harmondsworth 1969)
Stanley Payne, *Falange* (Stanford 1966)
* Hugh Thomas, *The Spanish Civil War* (Harmondsworth 1965)

List of illustrations

Special photography in the British Museum and the Victoria and Albert Museum by J. R. Freeman & Co.

Index